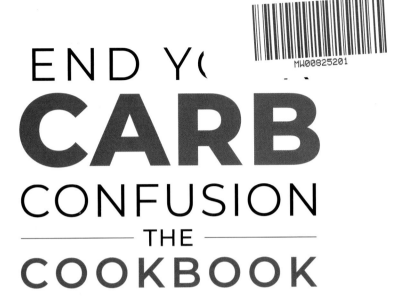

END YO CARB CONFUSION
THE
COOKBOOK

100 Carb-Customized Recipes from a Chef's Kitchen to Yours

SCOTT PARKER
with New York Times *Bestselling Author*
ERIC C. WESTMAN, MD

VICTORY BELT PUBLISHING INC.

LAS VEGAS

First published in 2022 by Victory Belt Publishing Inc.

Copyright © 2022 Scott Parker and Eric C. Westman

ISBN-13: 978-1-628604-63-4

Cover and interior design by Kat Lannom and Charisse Reyes

Interior illustrations by Kat Lannom, Eli San Juan, and Allan Santos

Food photography by Marguerite Oelofse

Food styling by Ellen Schwerdtfeger

Plates and cookware provided by Mervyn Gers and Le Creuset

Printed in Canada

TC 0122

CONTENTS

FOREWORD

I have known, worked with, and looked up to Scott for many years. When he first walked into my kitchen, he looked sharp as a knife with a clear understanding of where he wanted his career to go. He had worked at some of the best restaurants in the U.K.: Pied à Terre (two Michelin stars), Claude Bosi's Hibiscus (two Michelin stars), and Joël Robuchon's L'Atelier (two Michelin stars). With that background, I couldn't quite believe he was applying for a job at Midsummer House. From the minute I met Scott, his passion for food and great restaurants stood out. However, what struck me more was how much of a gentleman he is. He made me believe that we could achieve more together if he joined the team. At the time, he was working in London, and he had come up for one day to look at what we were doing but needed to catch a 10 p.m. train to get home. We got so engrossed in talking and cooking in that service that he missed his train, but this twist of serendipity gave me an opportunity to drive him to Stansted Airport and continue our conversation about him joining us.

Scott has worked for me on two different occasions—the first time was as sous chef. Later, he had an itch to go traveling around Asia and work in restaurants with three Michelin stars in Japan, and I did not want to hold him back. So Scott went off to Asia and worked in some amazing places. Eventually, he returned to the U.K. and joined me again—this time as head chef—and nothing could have pleased me more. Scott's true love is making food that makes people happy. I am pretty sure that is why he has gone into recipe development for retailers, which allows him to show off his skills to a much wider audience. When he left the second time, Scott made sure to train his replacement, Mark Abbott, to take over the responsibility and to run the kitchen as well as he had. (Mark remains the head chef of Midsummer House to this day, thanks in large part to Scott's guidance.)

When Scott was based in the U.K. and I needed trusted help with outside events, he was always my first call—not just for his talent in the kitchen but also because, when you're cooking away from home, it's great to have people by your side who make you happy. Scott has such a calming influence on me and makes me smile every time I speak to him. It would take a long time to tell you all the stories of the things we've done together and the unexpected adventures he's gotten me into. (Once, halfway through service, when we were sending 1,000 covers, he decided to steal a golf cart and begged me to go for a spin at the Henley Music Festival. Another time, he smooth-talked his way into Ronnie Scott's, a super-exclusive jazz club in London, when they didn't have a table, and suddenly there was a table for us right next to the stage.)

I've seen Scott grow as a chef and a person, and I've seen him get married and change direction in his career. However, the one thing that has never changed is his amazing personality and drive to help people. He now lives in South Africa, but we still speak on a regular basis. While maintaining a very stressful career, Scott has worked on projects to help school children to build new schools and new areas to grow ingredients. My life has been enriched by meeting Scott, and I am happy to call him a friend. In this book, you won't just see Scott in the pictures of the food; you will see a man who has spent his life loving the career that he carved for himself. Scott Fricker (now Parker), you are an absolute legend, and I love you to bits.

—Chef Daniel Clifford (Chef Patron, two-Michelin-starred Midsummer House)

INTRODUCTION

HELLO FROM THE CHEF

When Dr. Westman asked me to write this book, I didn't need to think twice. I've spent my life devoted to food: cooking it, eating it, judging it in competitions or for guides, developing recipes, getting into debt over it, traveling around the world in pursuit of it, and even dreaming about it. (Yes, even when I'm asleep, my brain still gravitates toward food!) I started cooking at the age of fifteen, when I spent most of my holidays and weekends working in my former stepdad's pub. I was lucky to have found a passion so early in my life. I was fortunate that my passion made for a viable profession, and that profession eventually evolved into an *obsession*.

I have worked in kitchens all over the world, from Japan to Denmark, the United Kingdom to South Africa—from casual spots to upscale restaurants with Michelin stars and, of course, in my home kitchen. The one constant throughout my career has been my *why*. I cook because I love making people happy. I lucked out that something I enjoy so much is a powerful way to do that. Food brings out people's emotions. One bite of something delicious can turn a stressful, taxing day around in a split second. A special meal shared in good company is the stuff of treasured memories you look back on and smile about for years to come. Cooking and eating together is one of the easiest ways to bond with other people. Food has the rare quality of being able to transcend politics, religion, and other contentious subjects and unite people around the table (well, okay, food can be pretty controversial, too!). Some of my fondest memories have been made at a dinner table. Reminiscing about my travels brings to mind images not of famous landmarks and historical sites but of the sights, smells, tastes, textures, and entire encompassing sensory experience of the foods I ate.

I was introduced to Dr. Westman by a mutual friend in South Africa. The low-carb, keto way of eating—"Banting," as we call it here—has been very popular in the last few years, so I was already familiar with the general concepts. It was a thrill to meet Dr. Westman, who was instrumental in the rebirth of scientific research to validate how effective keto is and who continues to see patients and help them change their lives through food. It was a no-brainer to say yes to writing this book. What chef wouldn't want to show people that food can be delicious *and* healthy, that you don't have to sacrifice flavor for nutrition, and, best of all, that dishes you'll love to eat can be simple and easy to prepare?

The recipes I've created for this book are easy to follow and clear in their nutritional content, so you can make sure you're eating the foods that work best for where you fall along the carb tolerance spectrum. Each recipe has been tested extensively, and I personally affirm that each one is delicious—or "lekker tasty," as we say in South Africa.

Even though I'm a professional chef, I don't like spending endless amounts of time fussing with long lists of hard-to-find ingredients and having to clear away and wash stacks of bowls, spoons, measuring cups, and special equipment. No, thank you; I'd rather be *cooking and eating*! I suspect you would, too, so these recipes are exactly the kinds of dishes I often cook for myself: fuss-free, with as little washing up as possible. The focus is on fresh, great-quality ingredients prepared simply.

I encourage you to muck up this book. If you get oily thumbprints or a smattering of sauce on the pages here and there, the more, the merrier! A pristine, unmarred cookbook is like a luxury sportscar with an odometer reading of zero. What's the point of that?! Take this book out for some joyrides! Be adventurous, even if it's only in your kitchen. Just be sure to stick to the recipes that match where you are in your carb tolerance: Phase 1, Phase 2, or Phase 3. Most of the recipes in this book are geared for Phase 1, but here and there, I've included modifications to increase the carbs for Phase 2 or 3. (It's pretty simple, honestly: just add a starch!) I have also included a chapter on some foundational techniques, like how to cook the perfect steak, roast a chicken, and make any style of eggs—scrambled, boiled, fried, poached, or omelette. These foundational recipes focus on classic technique rather than the "quick and easy" approach most of the others fall under. As a result, some take longer to prepare and cook, but they're skills you'll be glad to have in your culinary toolkit because once you've mastered them, you'll be able to apply them to all kinds of dishes, even without a recipe.

I hope you enjoy reading and using this book as much as I have loved writing it. I am humbled by the idea that I can help people use my favorite medium—food—to transform their health and their lives. I'm honored to play a role in your journey.

Make every meal memorable, and happy cooking!

—Scott Parker

A NOTE FROM DR. ERIC WESTMAN

You might be wondering why we made a companion cookbook to go along with *End Your Carb Confusion (EYCC)*. In *EYCC*, I make the point that the low-carb, keto way of eating is *simple*. You can make a meal out of deli counter roast beef and cucumber slices, and you can do perfectly well on the road stopping in at a gas station convenience store for some premade hard-boiled eggs, string cheese, and pepperoni. One of the things that draw people to keto is that you can get the results you want regardless of your budget or your desire to cook.

I've been helping people change their lives with this way of eating for over twenty years, and the patients who've come through my clinic are as diverse in their cooking skills as they are in their medical histories. Some of them are gourmet cooks who enjoy cooking elaborate menus from scratch in their home kitchens. Others didn't even own a *single pot or pan* and relied on restaurants and drive-thrus for all their meals. This is one of the great things about eating a low-carb or keto diet: you can do it successfully no matter your level of culinary skill.

You can have what my friend Dr. Mike Eades calls "down-home surf and turf" (canned tuna and pork rinds), or you can roast a prime rib and pair it with mashed cauliflower and homemade horseradish sauce. There are no rules or requirements except for one: stay within the daily carbohydrate limit that's appropriate for you.

You can be successful eating nothing but fast-food burger patties (minus the bun, of course) and salads. You can get a rotisserie chicken from a supermarket and pair it with premade zucchini noodles that you heat up in the microwave. In fact, in *End Your Carb Confusion*, I point out that the reason there are no recipes, shopping lists, or meal plans is that it's so easy to eat this way without a plan! If you stick to the food list for the phase you're in and stay within your carb tolerance, you don't have to weigh or measure your food, count calories, or track anything in an app. It's critical that you stay within your daily carb limit, but if you follow the food list for your phase, you don't even have to count carbs! Sticking to the list will ensure you're exactly where you need to be. (See Appendix B for the EYCC food lists.)

But I know some of you have more adventurous palates, and you like to keep things exciting in the kitchen. Just because you might not *need* new recipes and ideas doesn't mean it's not nice to have them. Bacon and eggs are delicious, but it is possible to get tired of them. Plus, you might have an easier time *sticking with this way of eating* for the long term if you keep things varied and interesting. And that's key. This isn't a short-term, quick-fix crash diet that you pull out of your pocket once or twice a year to drop a few pounds before a vacation or reunion. This is a life-saving metabolic therapy that just so happens to work through eating delicious food.

If you are already a good cook, eating keto or low carb doesn't mean you have to overhaul your entire culinary repertoire. All you need to do is eliminate the sweet and starchy ingredients; it's as simple as that. For example, if you were accustomed to serving roasted chicken with baked potatoes, keep the chicken and just substitute mashed cauliflower or roasted radishes for the potatoes. Your family likes meatloaf? Simply leave out the breadcrumbs—they're not necessary. But if you prefer the texture of a meatloaf that has a binder in it, use crushed pork rinds instead of breadcrumbs. (I did say this was simple, right?)

I'll tell you a little more about low-carb and keto diets in the next section. I'll also give you a quick overview of the three phases of carbohydrate intake from *End Your Carb Confusion* so you'll understand why certain ingredients are included in Chef Scott's recipes and others are absent. (If you've already read *EYCC*, it'll be a quick review, and if you're brand-new to all of this, it'll be just enough information to get you started.)

Then I'll hand things over to Chef Scott, a culinary professional who understands that cutting carbs doesn't mean cutting flavor and knows that you can lose weight and restore your health without sacrificing delight and decadence at the table.

Why Do Carbs Matter?

Keeping your blood sugar and insulin levels within a healthy range is one of the most important things you can do to stay healthy for life. When you hear the words *blood sugar* and *insulin*, you probably think about diabetes, especially type 2 diabetes (T2D). But T2D is only the tip of the iceberg—a very large iceberg—when it comes to health issues rooted in chronically high blood sugar and/or insulin. For example, polycystic ovarian syndrome (PCOS), which affects millions of women, is driven by chronically high insulin. Metabolic syndrome, non-alcoholic fatty liver disease, hypertension, gout, skin tags, and migraines are just a handful of the issues caused or worsened by constantly high blood sugar or insulin. Even cardio-vascular disease—it's not caused by eating red meat, bacon, butter, or any kind of saturated fat or animal food. Cardiovascular disease is the number one cause of death in people with T2D, and it has a lot more to do with damage to the heart muscle and blood vessels caused by high blood sugar and insulin than it does with animal fats "clogging" the arteries.

We spend billions of dollars in the U.S. on managing or treating T2D. If we factor in the whole world, we're talking about trillions of dollars used for medication, dialysis, special socks and shoes, and other things that make the symptoms look a little better on paper but do nothing to address the disease itself. I'm here to tell you that you don't have to "manage" T2D. You can be free of it entirely. Reverse it. Put it into remission. *Get rid of it altogether.*

Because constantly high blood sugar and insulin are the main culprits behind so many chronic health issues, the key goal is to bring these levels down. And the most effective way to do so is to stop consuming the foods and beverages that raise them the most: those that contain carbohydrates.

Most of my patients see heartburn disappear within a few days of starting a keto diet, even if they continue to drink their morning coffee and keep spicy or acidic foods in their diet, like chili peppers and tomato sauce. These things typically get the blame for heartburn and acid reflux, but the truth is, for most people, it's sugars and starches that cause the problem! Joint pain improves fairly quickly as well—long before someone loses a lot of weight. This tells us that it's not just the burden of carrying extra weight that causes pain in the joints and muscles; it's internal inflammation from high blood sugar and insulin. And of course, once your blood sugar is stable and you're not experiencing wild fluctuations on the blood sugar roller coaster, all the brain fog, irritability, and mood swings from hypoglycemia will disappear, too.

With regard to medicines, cutting carbs is so powerful and works so quickly that I sometimes have to reduce or stop a patient's insulin injections altogether on the *very first day* they start a low-carb or ketogenic diet. (Think about it: if someone takes the same dose of insulin they needed when they were eating a lot of carbs, they'll end up in a dangerous situation of having low blood sugar now that they're eating hardly any. Someone with the autoimmune type of diabetes—type 1—will always need at least a small amount of insulin, but they, too, can reduce their doses when they eat this way.) Other issues that get better when people cut back on their carb intake are high blood pressure, skin issues (acne, eczema, psoriasis, skin tags, and so on), and even PMS.

Insulin injections aren't the only things that need to be reduced or stopped as the body heals on a low-carb diet. When acid reflux disappears, antacids can be cut out. Likewise, when joint pain and other types of inflammation are ameliorated, doses and frequency of pain relievers can be reduced, too. I also regularly reduce or eliminate blood pressure medication for my patients. (A small number of people are sensitive to sodium, and when they eat a lot of salt, their blood pressure goes up. For most people, however, it's actually excess carbs that drive hypertension.)

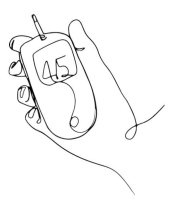

As you can see, strict ketogenic diets are extremely powerful. They do what medications cannot and will never be able to do. Medications help manage symptoms; *keto corrects the underlying problems.*

I see it in my clinic every day. I've been seeing it for over two decades, and I'm *still* sometimes amazed at the transformations my patients achieve—just by changing their food! I've gotten people with T2D off of *hundreds of units of insulin* within just a few days of starting a keto diet.

And yet, as amazing as keto is, not everyone needs to eat this way. There are billions of healthy people all over the world who include generous amounts of carbohydrates in their diets, and they're perfectly healthy. So what gives? How can it be true that some people can eat fruit, beans, grains, and other sweet and starchy foods while remaining lean and healthy, whereas others do best eating little to none of those?

It's pretty simple, actually—the more extreme your health situation, the stricter an approach you need to turn it around. If you fall into the deep end of a pool but you can't swim, you don't want to wait and see if you'll magically drift across to the shallow side where you can put your feet down and simply stand up. You want the lifeguard to pull you out, *stat*! What does that have to do with keto? Other ways of eating can work to help you lose weight and get healthier, but so far, keto has more scientific evidence in its favor than any other approach. And the best part is, I've seen it work for thousands of people with no calorie counting and no superhuman feats of willpower. You don't have to deprive yourself and go hungry when you eat keto. You can eat; just keep the carbs low!

But all of this doesn't mean everyone needs strict keto. I wrote *End Your Carb Confusion* to be useful for all people, no matter where they fall along the spectrum of carbohydrate tolerance. Some people do best with keto, keeping carbs to a bare minimum. Others can get the results they want by cutting back on carbs a little but being more generous with them than on a strict keto plan. People who are healthy, lean, and active tend to have the most flexibility with regard to carbohydrate intake. Still, even for them, inundating the body with sugar and starch all day, every day is not the greatest idea.

Which Phase Is Right for You?

You probably already know which phase of carb intake is right for you, but if you haven't read *End Your Carb Confusion* and you need to figure this out, the quiz in Appendix A will point you in the right direction. You'll find complete food lists and guidelines for each of the three phases in Appendix B, but here's a quick overview.

PHASE ① STRICT KETO

20 total grams of carbohydrate per day or fewer

Phase 1 is what I call "prescription-strength keto." I use this phrase to distinguish it from "internet keto," which has several drawbacks. It's wonderful that so many people are sharing information about this way of eating on social media. However, the majority of these people are not medical or nutrition professionals, so myths and misinformation are rampant. In the past couple of years, I have spent more time than ever before busting these myths and setting the record straight with my patients. The goal is to help people do keto in the simple, uncomplicated, inexpensive, and effective way I've been teaching for twenty years.

At just 20 total grams of carbohydrate per day or fewer, Phase 1 is a therapeutic diet. Eating this way can help reverse obesity, type 2 diabetes (it's also dynamite for improving blood sugar control in type 1), PCOS, non-alcoholic fatty liver disease, heartburn, and more. To say that Phase 1 is as powerful as medication would be an understatement because, as I mentioned earlier, it's actually *more* powerful than medicine. Instead of just masking the symptoms, strict keto, as outlined in Phase 1, reverses the disease process itself. You don't have to manage symptoms when you don't have any symptoms, and you don't have symptoms because you're free of the condition altogether! I will say this: if the Phase 1 food list were a prescription drug, the evidence of its safety and effectiveness would be so robust and undeniable that it undoubtedly would be approved by the U.S. Food and Drug Administration (FDA).

When following Phase 1, you may consume as much as you like of certain zero-carb or close-to-zero-carb foods until you are comfortably full. These include any cuts of animal proteins—beef, bison, lamb, pork, poultry, eggs, seafood, and game meats—as long as there's no starchy breading or batter. As you'll see on the Phase 1 food list in Appendix B, foods that do have carbohydrates, such as nonstarchy vegetables, are limited. Very concentrated sources of fat—like cheese, butter, oils, and heavy cream—are permitted in limited quantities. Even though these foods are very low in carbs, they're dense in fat, and overdoing added fats and oils is one of the most common roadblocks that get in the way of weight loss. (If you've come across the abbreviation LCHF for a low-carb, high-fat diet, keep in mind that if your main goal is to lose body fat, the *LC* part is more important than the *HF*. What makes this way of eating so powerful is the absence of carbs, not an abundance of fat.)

REMEMBER:
20 grams of carbs is a limit to stay under every day; it's not a target you need to hit. It's okay to be under 20 grams.

PHASE ② **VERY LOW CARB**

50 total grams of carbohydrate per day or fewer

At 50 grams of carbohydrate per day or fewer, Phase 2 is a very-low-carb diet. For some people, it is even ketogenic. Everyone differs in how much carbohydrate they can consume and still be in a ketogenic state. Some people need to keep things really low, like in Phase 1, but others can be a little more liberal with carbs and remain in ketosis. But being in ketosis doesn't matter much anyway. What matters is whether you're getting the results you want. The goal isn't to be in ketosis; the goal is to be happy with your health and how you look and feel.

Most people can reap the benefits of a low-carb diet by following Phase 2. Phase 2 is also where many will remain for the long term after achieving their health and weight goals on Phase 1. Although the Phase 2 food list allows for a bit more carbohydrate, most people find that they can still keep their blood sugar and insulin levels within a healthy range. In addition, they can enjoy a wider variety of foods on Phase 2 than on Phase 1 without regaining weight or having a recurrence of health problems.

The Phase 2 food list includes everything on the Phase 1 list, plus some foods that are slightly higher in carbs, such as berries, yogurt, winter squash, some root vegetables, nuts, and seeds.

REMEMBER:
50 grams of carbs is a limit to stay under every day; it's not a target you need to hit. It's okay to be under 50 grams.

150 total grams of carbohydrate per day or fewer

Phase 3 is the most generous with regard to carbohydrate. No foods are off-limits, but it's not an unregulated carb free-for-all. People who appear to be at the pinnacle of health on the outside are not immune to metabolic disease on the inside. Even professional athletes aren't automatically protected from blood sugar problems and insulin resistance.

Phase 3 is the right level for lean and healthy people who have little to no family history of major chronic illness. Very active people may find that they feel best with the higher amount of carbohydrate permitted on Phase 3. However, it's worth noting that many elite athletes have adopted lower-carb diets and are surpassing their previous performance levels and setting new personal bests. The dogma about carb loading before a race is a thing of the past.

With a limit of 150 total grams of carbohydrate per day, Phase 3 allows for starchy vegetables, beans, and grains. However, it's still relatively low in carbs compared to what some people eat on an unrestricted or standard Western diet. For example, if you have toast with jam, a bowl of cereal with skim milk, and a glass of orange juice for breakfast, you can get close to 100 grams of carbs from your first meal of the day alone!

At 4 calories per gram, 150 grams of carbohydrate provides 600 calories—not all that much for an active person. Nevertheless, if you're following Phase 3, you might choose to stick to the lower-carb side of things most of the time and reserve higher-carb days for when you're training hard, or opt to consume most of your carb-dense choices during your post-workout meals.

REMEMBER:
150 grams of carbs is a limit to stay under every day; it's not a target you need to hit. It's okay to be under 150 grams.

A Word About the Recipes

You will notice that a few of the recipes call for individual ingredients that are not technically included in the food list for that phase: for example, the almond and coconut flours in the Two-Minute Cheese and Chive Rolls on page 58 for Phase 1, and the apple in the Five-Minute Salmon on page 156 for Phase 2. The total amounts of these ingredients are small and should not interfere with the progress you are making in weight loss or with regard to your health. As I explain in *End Your Carb Confusion*, things like nuts and seeds are prohibited on Phase 1 not because they are high in carbs but because they are common trigger foods that many people have difficulty keeping to reasonable portions. It may be easier to have none of these foods at all than to try to limit the quantity. As a result, to make Phase 1 as effective as possible for the largest number of people, I chose to leave nuts and seeds off the list entirely.

It's up to you to decide whether it's suitable for you to keep those ingredients on hand for the recipes that call for them or whether doing so would ultimately lead to self-sabotage and move you further from your goals. Remember, the food lists are intended to keep your total carbohydrate intake under a certain limit for the day; they're not commandments carved in stone. Some degree of flexibility is built in, and beyond that, you are free to experiment to see what gets you the results you want.

A Note About Medication

Low-carb diets—especially a strict keto approach like Phase 1—are very effective, and they will begin to affect your body quickly. If you are taking medication for diabetes (either type 1 or type 2) or high blood pressure, it's essential that you work with your doctor so that you understand *ahead of time* when and how to adjust your medication should the need arise.

This is especially critical if you use insulin injections for diabetes. When your carbohydrate intake is very low, you cannot use the same dose of insulin you were accustomed to when your carb intake was much higher or you will risk having a dangerous hypoglycemic event (low blood sugar). The risks are not quite as extreme with blood pressure medicine. Still, because keto helps normalize blood pressure naturally, your blood pressure might eventually become too low when you combine the diet with medication. If this happens, you may become sluggish, woozy, dizzy, or light-headed, or you could faint. If you take medication for diabetes or blood pressure and you start to feel unwell, consult your doctor to adjust the dose. Don't blame the diet for what the medication is doing!

And now, I'll turn things over to Scott. I can teach you the science of keto, but I know my limits. If you want some ideas for cooking keto, you don't want someone in a white lab coat; you want someone in a white chef's jacket!

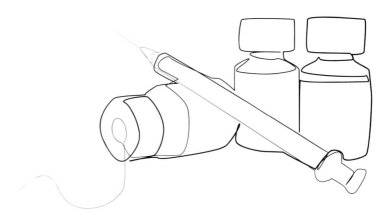

HOW TO USE THIS BOOK

Each recipe is color-coded to make it easier to find the ones that fit your phase of carbohydrate intake. The recipes are intentionally weighted heavily toward Phase 1 because I wanted to offer as many options as possible to the widest range of people. Those following Phase 1 are advised to avoid the Phase 2 and 3 recipes, but those on Phase 2 or 3 (with or without an added starch) can enjoy all of the Phase 1 recipes. The majority of the recipes are Phase 1–friendly for this reason.

The recipes include breakfasts, appetizers, main dishes, sides, soups, salads, a few snacks, and some staples like broths and seasoning blends. I've also included a guide to "the perfect" method for making a handful of classic dishes. It's easy to mix and match things to tailor your meals to the phase you're following. Each recipe is another tool in your toolkit to help you put together meals that suit your needs. Some recipes include suggestions for making them suitable for other phases, as you may be cooking for people who are not at the same level of carb intake you are. Nobody should have to prepare unique meals for every individual and be a short-order cook in their own home!

Most of the recipes are intended to serve one person because I know it's a rare household in which everyone eats keto or low carb. Often, it's just one individual doing it on their own. However, all of the recipes can be made in larger quantities if you are one of the lucky ones whose family members eat the same way you do, or if you'd simply prefer to make bigger batches to have a few days' worth of meals for yourself prepped in advance. Alternatively, you can test out a recipe for yourself the first time you make it and, if it's a winner, make it again sometime for the whole family. (Hopefully, you'll want to make them lots of times!)

EQUIPMENT LIST

Here's a list of equipment that I find instrumental to cooking and recommend you keep handy in the kitchen to make the recipes in this book. Of course, there are thousands of utensils, gadgets and gizmos, and expensive devices and contraptions that you could outfit a kitchen with, but the truth is, to make phenomenal yet simple food at home, all you need are a few basics. Pricey machines may look nice on your counter, but what often happens is that these become like the treadmill you bought and swore you were going to use five times a week: it just sits there unused, collecting dust.

I've steered clear of tools such as vacuum sealers, liquid nitrogen, foaming cartridges, and salamander broilers, which are essential in fine-dining restaurant kitchens but hardly necessary at home. Things like sea urchin mousse and squid ink gels are best left to TV cooking competitions. For your home kitchen, let's keep it real, keep it old-school, and keep it simple. I've included a few recipes that work best on an outdoor grill, but a good old-fashioned skillet and a humble pot will get you through most of this book. This list is not exhaustive; I assume you've got some cutting boards and mixing bowls in a variety of sizes, plus some utensils for cooking and serving—such as wooden spoons, a spatula, rubber scraper (aka rubber spatula), whisk, ladle, slotted spoon/spider strainer, kitchen shears, and so on. I will highlight the key points of what you need to know about the most basic items, such as knives and pots and pans, as well as some less common but highly useful items.

Knives

Knives can become quite an expensive hobby for chefs and advanced home cooks. However, the reality is you only need a few well-made knives. You don't need to break the bank to buy them, and if you take good care of them, they will last a long time. I still have two Victorinox knives—the type with a wooden handle—that I bought when I started cooking nearly twenty years ago!

Get yourself a sturdy chef's knife—an 8-inch (20cm) one will cover all your bases. You will also need a paring knife for smaller cuts and peeling and a slicing and carving knife to carve up all the amazing roasts in this book. Store your knives well by using a knife block to protect the blades and sharpen them regularly using steel or a whetstone, and they will last you a lifetime.

Strainers and Sieves

I use strainers a lot at home to strain broths, pureed soups, and even mashed vegetables to make sure they're silky smooth. A chinois, which is a cone-shaped sieve made of fine metal mesh, is typically used in fine-dining restaurant kitchens to strain stocks, sauces, and soups. However, it's quite spendy and rather hard to find. A sturdy fine-mesh strainer or sieve, lined with a piece of slightly dampened muslin or cheesecloth, will do just fine for catching any impurities or sediment when you pass homemade stocks or broths through it.

Tongs and Tweezers

These tools are great when frying foods over high heat to avoid any fat splashing back and burning your hands, and they work wonders when cooking over a BBQ grill. I use different sizes depending on what I'm cooking: tongs for larger items and tweezers for smaller ones.

Digital Food Scale

I highly recommend a reliable digital kitchen scale because measuring ingredients by weight (ounces or grams) is more precise than measuring by volume (cups and tablespoons). The recipes in this book have been finely calibrated to suit the carb level for each phase of *End Your Carb Confusion*, and the accuracy of the nutritional data—not to mention the success of the recipes—depends on this level of precision. For some people, eating a few extra grams of carbohydrate here and there isn't a problem, but for others, it can mean the difference between nearly effortless weight loss and a stall, or well-controlled blood sugar versus not. Using precise measurements removes the guesswork.

When it comes to scales, you often get what you pay for, so this isn't the place to cut corners. When you're trying to be precise with your ingredients, it's worth investing in a high-quality food scale.

Be sure to use the tare function: if you are weighing ingredients in a bowl or some other container rather than directly on the scale's surface, put the empty container on the scale first. Hitting the tare button at this point will zero out the weight of the container. Then put your ingredient in the container and weigh it so that your measurement will be accurate. It's an extra step, but it takes only seconds.

Mandoline

Sometimes called a Japanese slicer, a mandoline is used to cut food into slices or shreds of even size and thickness with a quickness, precision, and ease that would be difficult to achieve by hand. A good mandoline should be sturdy and have a slicing guard to protect your hands. Look for one that has a removable blade; that way, you can replace it when it goes blunt and it's easier to keep clean. Some mandolines have adjustable settings for different thicknesses. I use a Benriner, but there are plenty of other options available, including a V-slicer and even a julienne peeler.

 Regardless of which type you get, use it with great caution, as the blade is surgically sharp. Always use the guard that came with the mandoline or wear a cut-resistant glove. I've seen many a finger succumb to the blade of the notorious mandoline!

Microplane Grater

A Microplane is a thin metal grater used for grating ingredients extra finely. (This tool is technically a rasp, but many people know it by the brand name Microplane.) It is often used to grate chunks of hard cheeses, like aged Parmesan; it is also one of the best tools for zesting citrus fruits. Several recipes in this book call for lemon or lime zest, which is the very thin, outermost layer of the fruit's rind. It's loaded with flavor and fragrance and adds an incredible zing that makes dishes brighter and livelier while adding nearly zero carbs. A Microplane will help you remove only the flavorful and aromatic zest while avoiding the pith, the bitter white part of the citrus peel below. (Keep in mind that it's always easier to grate the zest before you cut the fruit in half, so zest first and then cut.) It's worth purchasing a Microplane for zesting citrus fruits because a conventional cheese grater will not allow you to grate the zest as finely as needed.

Food Processor, High-Powered Blender, and Immersion Blender

Not many recipes in this book require a food processor, but it's a must if you plan to make the mashed vegetable or soup recipes. For mashed vegetables, you can use a handheld potato masher if you prefer (and if you want a hard-core arm workout), but you won't achieve the creamy, smooth mouthfeel or the appetizing velvety finish.

In addition to a food processor, I recommend a high-powered blender and an immersion blender. The use of high-powered blenders to create smooth purees and soups used to be limited to professional restaurant kitchens, but now these heavy-duty tools are readily available to home cooks. These blenders don't come cheap, but they are built to be more durable and reliable than regular blenders, and their horsepower and blades can turn grains into flours, nuts and seeds into butters, and even the toughest, most fibrous vegetables into creamy purees. Blending Broccoli, Spinach, and Stilton Soup (page 86) or Cauliflower Cheese and Pancetta Soup (page 88) silky smooth is simple with the help of this powerful machine.

I also recommend that you get an immersion blender (aka stick blender), as it will make blending foods, especially hot foods, so much easier due to its ability to blend directly in a saucepan or pot. Its simple and sleek construction also allows you to blend in a wide-mouthed jar or even a glass measuring cup. For example, to make homemade mayonnaise (see the recipe on page 208), you can simply put all of the ingredients in a quart (liter)-sized mason jar and use an immersion blender to blend everything—right in the jar!—into beautifully emulsified mayonnaise, which you can store in the same jar. Also, the slender blender requires no precious countertop real estate for storage; you can simply stash it in a kitchen drawer.

Pots and Pans

You will see throughout the book that I use Le Creuset's high-quality enameled cast-iron pots and pans. There is a good reason most professional chefs don't skimp on cookware: reliability. Cast iron conducts heat well and evenly; it doesn't buckle and bow over high heat, meaning your food will cook in a consistent manner. This is particularly important when, for example, you want an evenly browned crust on a steak (see page 226).

I have used plenty of pots and pans made with other materials over the years but found that they are inferior and simply don't last as long. In terms of performance, only copper cookware can compete with cast iron, but it also costs a small fortune.

A good nonstick skillet is also a must. It comes in handy for some of the egg recipes in this book, namely the perfect fried eggs (see page 260) and the perfect omelette (see page 261), and for cooking skin-on fish fillets evenly, both getting the delicate skin super crispy and keeping it intact. Look for nonstick pans with a thicker base, as they conduct heat far better, won't warp, and tend to last longer than thin, flimsy ones.

Grill Pan

A grill pan is a fantastic cooking vessel, particularly for people who live in apartments or don't have an outdoor grill. It will impart not only the enticing grill marks—thanks to the raised ridges across the cooking surface—on a piece of meat, fish, or grilled vegetables but also a great charred flavor. I recommend that you use one made from cast iron or enameled cast iron because it can withstand high temperatures and retains heat well.

Thermometer

This is a great tool to ensure your food is cooked precisely to the temperature you want every time; if you want to ensure meat, especially larger cuts, is cooked perfectly, get one of these. There are so many options on the market nowadays. The more expensive ones are faster—and likely more accurate—at reading temperatures, but you can pick up a reliable one at a more modest price.

Note that even a good thermometer doesn't stay reliable over time; being dropped on the floor too often, for example, can affect a thermometer's accuracy. Therefore, it's a good idea to calibrate a thermometer right after you buy it and after having used it for a while. A good calibration test is to dip the stem in boiling water to see if it's at 212°F (100°C), or fill up a glass with ice, top it off with cold water, and insert the stem into it to make sure the thermometer reads 32°F (0°C). It's important to do this every so often to ensure your thermometer is working optimally.

A WELL-STOCKED PANTRY

It's possible to follow a low-carb or keto diet consisting mostly of very mild, unseasoned foods, but where's the fun in that? Eating bland food all the time would be like wearing the same color from head to toe every day—a total snooze-fest! Generous use of herbs and spices will bring your food to life while contributing only a negligible amount of carbs. As a professional chef, I can tell you that restaurant food sometimes tastes better than home-cooked food because the pros aren't afraid to season. If you're going to stick with your lower-carb way of eating for the long term, then the food's got to be delicious. It doesn't matter how effective an eating plan is if the food straight-up doesn't taste good; no one is going to stay with it if the food is boring. Proper seasoning can make all the difference.

You'll want to have salt in the pantry at all times. I always have at least three types on hand:

- Table salt is great for seasoning water when you blanch or cook vegetables or make my All-Purpose Brine (page 268); it's the cheapest for use in larger quantities. It's a salt that has been mined.

- I use sea salt, a salt extracted from the ocean, for recipes like kimchi and pickles because it has a better flavor.

- Maldon salt, a brand of flaky sea salt, deserves to be called out all by itself. I can't imagine life without those tiny little flakes whose greatness will elevate pretty much any dish. I use Maldon salt as a finishing touch to provide a surprising little crunch. The fact that it comes from my native county of Essex, England, makes it feel like a touch of home to me.

I also recommend that you keep fresh black peppercorns on hand and use a mill or grinder, which should be inexpensive and widely available, to make freshly ground pepper. The flavor of freshly ground or cracked pepper is a world apart from the fine, powdery pepper in that little metal tin that's lost much of its potency after having sat in a warehouse, then on a store shelf, and finally in your cupboard.

It's also a good idea to keep onions and garlic on hand. Keep them dry at room temperature, and they'll last a while.

Other seasonings worth having around and used in this book are

- Bay leaves
- Coriander seeds
- Cumin seeds
- Ginger powder
- Paprika
- Star anise

You can buy some of these spices ground, but if you buy them whole and grind them yourself, you'll find they're much more fragrant. A small coffee grinder works wonderfully. (If you use a coffee grinder, invest in one that you use solely for this purpose. You don't want your morning coffee tasting like cumin!)

Having fresh herbs around also makes things easier in the kitchen. You can use dried herbs in a pinch if that's all you have on hand, but fresh herbs will give a dish a better flavor (they make beautiful garnishes, too).

Other key pantry ingredients you'll want to keep stocked are

- Red wine vinegar
- White wine vinegar
- Unseasoned rice vinegar (not to be confused with the sugar-laden seasoned variety)
- Olive oil (regular and extra-virgin)
- Toasted sesame oil (I prefer toasted sesame oil for finishing because it has a better aroma and taste; plain [untoasted] sesame oil is better for cooking with, however, as it has a higher smoke point.)

Lastly, even though this is not exactly a pantry ingredient, it's something you may want to have: zoodles. These "noodles" are made from finely sliced zucchini. You can make them yourself by using a spiral slicer, a julienne peeler, or a knife, but they are now conveniently available in most supermarkets, either fresh or frozen. Zoodles are an excellent low-carb substitute for spaghetti or other pasta in noodle dishes, such as Zoodle Bolognese (page 148) and Dad's Singapore Zoodles (page 100).

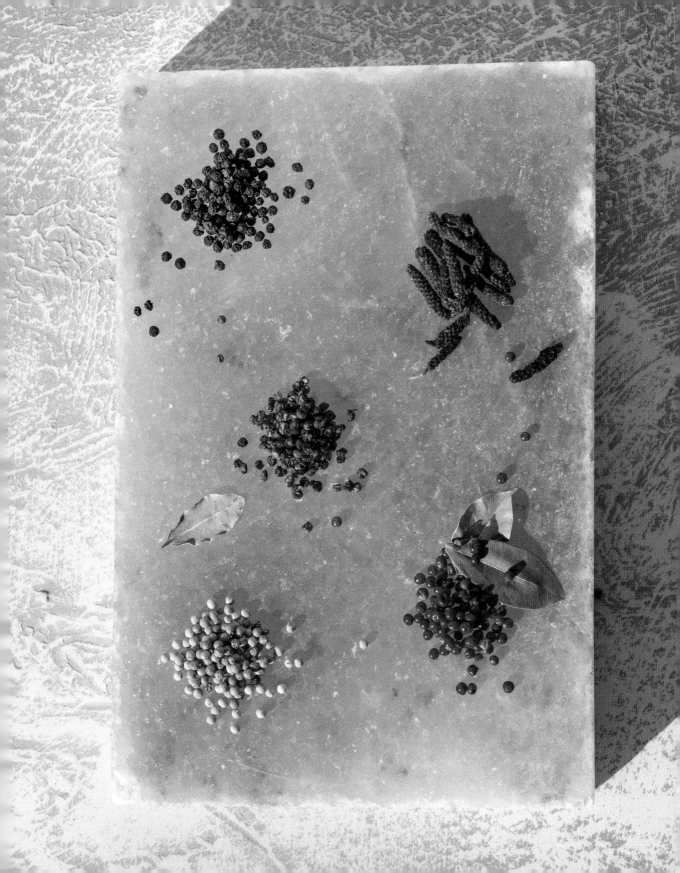

COOKING AND EATING TOGETHER

As mentioned before, food has a wonderful way of bringing people together. I can't tell you how much joy it brings me to have a dinner table full of happy people chatting and laughing. This really is when I'm at my happiest, surrounded by family and friends.

Food is an international language that everyone can speak. The recipes in this book are not just for those who are looking to follow a low-carb or keto diet, but rather for anyone who is keen on cooking great food that can bring people together. The secret to this is simple: I always source fresh, in-season ingredients that are as local to me as possible. I prepare them simply and serve them with other dishes that enhance their natural flavor. You will see this in this book. Remember, when you buy in-season and local ingredients, more often than not they will cost far less than that oversized Peruvian asparagus that was cut down last month before being flown halfway around the world to end up on your plate. Not to mention that this is exactly what's adding to our global climate crisis.

Cooking for large numbers can be daunting (I think a combination of that and my being a chef is why I don't get invited around to other people's homes often!), but it really doesn't need to be. My top tips for entertaining that will help you prepare for your next dinner party, barbecue, or other gathering are as follows:

- Always plan ahead: make sure you know what you want to cook, how you are going to cook it, and what you are going to serve it with.

- Get the shopping done early to avoid that panic when you get to stores and they don't have some of the ingredients you needed.

- Do what you can ahead of time: marinate meats, roast vegetables, and prep cauliflower rice. The last thing you want to be doing when everyone turns up for a party is running around trying to say howzit to Nanny Pat while spiralizing a zucchini.

- Finally, less is more. You don't need to serve five to ten dishes; it's not a tasting menu. Keep it simple and focus on two or three great dishes: a protein (see the Foundations chapter) and then one or two sides followed by a dessert. Cheese is your best mate here; it's a wonderful way to end a low-carb/keto meal. Just be sure to remove it from the fridge an hour before you want to serve it so it is at its optimal temperature.

RECIPES

BREAKFAST

All of the recipes in this chapter include eggs, but don't let that fool you. When you follow a low-carb or a ketogenic diet—or any other way of eating, for that matter—you don't need to stick only to what you think of as conventional "breakfast foods" for your first meal of the day. Eggs, sausages, and bacon are great, but the truth is, you can have just about anything you like for breakfast as long as you stay within your carb tolerance. Leftovers make great breakfasts, especially when you're in a hurry. Grab some cold leftover poached chicken (see page 246) and dip it in one of the sauces or dressings you made. Or pop a few leftover frikkadels (page 54) into a container to take with you to eat on the go. You could even have a can of sardines or salmon; it doesn't have to be complicated. If you do prefer something a little more traditional, however, the recipes in this chapter have you covered.

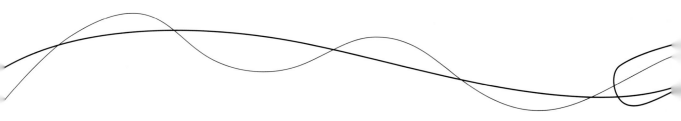

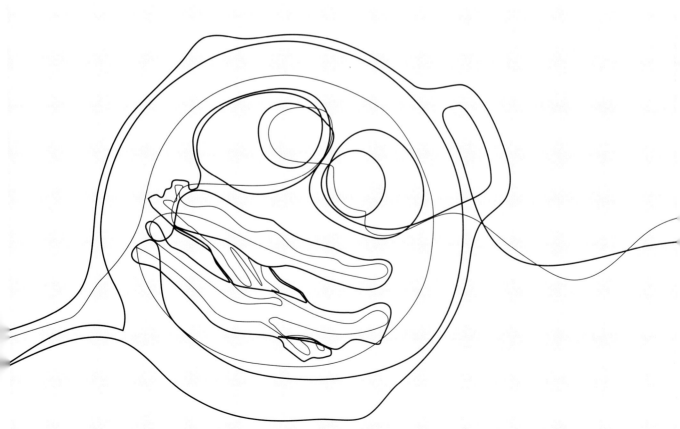

PROSCIUTTO, CHEESE, AND VEGGIE EGG ROLL

SERVES 1

No, not like an egg roll from your favorite Chinese takeout place. This one is keto-friendly and will give you protein and fat to get your day started. It's quick and easy to make, and you can fill it with just about anything. I use fresh baby spinach here. However, hardier greens, like Swiss chard, lightly sautéed in a little bit of butter and roughly chopped, will work just as well, as will bell peppers, mushrooms, onions, or shallots. Feel free to experiment! Consider cooking up a big batch on a weekend so you can enjoy one for breakfast and keep a few more in the fridge to grab on your way out the door on hectic weekday mornings. Great hot or cold, these egg rolls make a perfect healthy snack, too, even for people who eat higher-carb diets.

1 tablespoon unsalted butter

2 large eggs

Salt and fresh ground black pepper

¼ cup (10g) fresh baby spinach

2 tablespoons grated Parmesan cheese

2 slices prosciutto

1 tablespoon thinly sliced jalapeño or other green chili pepper

Maldon salt, for finishing (optional)

1. Melt the butter in a large nonstick skillet over medium heat.

2. Crack the eggs into a bowl, season with a pinch each of salt and pepper, and whisk into a smooth, cohesive mixture, about 1 minute. Add the eggs to the pan and cook until the bottom is set but the top is still glossy, about 90 seconds.

3. Lay the spinach across the egg, followed by the Parmesan and then the prosciutto and jalapeño. Gently roll the egg around the filling. (Be careful; it'll be hot.)

4. Remove from the pan, slice, and serve immediately. Sprinkle with Maldon salt, if desired.

Nutrition:		
Carb	Fat	Protein
2.8g	42.1g	26.1g

BREAKFAST STACK

SERVES 1

A protein- and flavor-packed way to start your day, minus the carbs. This dish is admittedly a bit calorie-dense for the first meal of the day, but with the cheese, bacon, egg, and avocado, it will help you stay satiated and energized for several hours. It's the perfect breakfast for a big day when you're busy and might not have a chance to eat again until the evening.

---

3 strips bacon, cut in half crosswise

3.5 ounces (100g) halloumi cheese

Salt and fresh ground black pepper

⅔ cup (30g) fresh spinach

2 tablespoons kale pesto, homemade (page 214) or store-bought

2 ounces (50g) thin slices avocado

1 large egg, fried (see page 260)

Maldon salt, for finishing (optional)

1. Fry the bacon in a medium-sized nonstick skillet over medium-high heat until crispy. Remove from the pan and place on a paper towel to drain, preferably in a warm place. (In the oven on a low setting is perfect.) Keep the bacon fat in the skillet and turn the heat up to high.

2. Season the halloumi cheese with a pinch each of salt and pepper, then place it in the skillet with the bacon fat and brown on all sides, 30 to 60 seconds per side. Once the cheese is browned, remove it from the pan and place it with the bacon to stay warm.

3. While still on the heat, add the spinach to the skillet, season with a pinch each of salt and pepper, and leave to wilt for about 1 minute. Remove from the pan and place with the rest of the components.

4. To serve, spread the pesto in the center of a serving plate, then add the spinach, avocado, halloumi, and bacon. Top with the fried egg. If desired, finish with a pinch each of Maldon salt and pepper.

Nutrition:		
Carb	Fat	Protein
10.7g	67.9g	51.8g

POACHED EGGS WITH FETA ON CHEESE AND CHIVE TOAST

SERVES 1

Who doesn't love poached eggs on toast? Add some ham and cheese and you've got a meal that's nutritious and high in protein but light enough that you'll feel nourished and ready to tackle the day rather than bogged down. This variation is one of my favorites. The sweet and salty feta helps balance the richness of the eggs (you can use unmarinated feta if needed), and on a crispy piece of toast, there's a ton of textural interest, too. And to top it all off, it looks amazing!

1 Two-Minute Cheese and Chive Roll (page 58)

2 slices prosciutto

2 large eggs, poached (see page 254)

½ cup (100g) Marinated Feta Cheese (page 60)

6 fresh basil leaves, roughly torn

Fresh ground black pepper

1. Cut the roll in half horizontally and toast the halves in a dry skillet over medium-high heat or in a toaster oven until warmed through on the inside and crisp on the outside.

2. Arrange the rolls and prosciutto on a serving plate. Top each roll with a poached egg. Scatter the marinated feta on top, followed by the basil and a pinch of pepper. Serve immediately.

Nutrition:		
Carb	Fat	Protein
8.9g	70.9g	64.3g

SMOKED SALMON OMELETTE

SERVES 1

Give ham and cheese a break sometimes. An omelette can feature any ingredients you like. This is an upscale version with smoked salmon that will have you feeling like you're in a gourmet restaurant in your own home. Not a fan of salmon? Use any other smoked fish you enjoy. You can substitute a different microgreen or even arugula for the watercress. Read more about omelettes on page 261.

3 large eggs

¼ teaspoon plus 1 pinch of salt

3 tablespoons olive oil, divided

2 ounces (50g) smoked salmon, sliced into strips, plus more for garnish if desired

3 tablespoons (20g) shredded cheddar cheese

1 cup (15g) watercress

Fresh ground black pepper, for finishing (optional)

Maldon salt, for finishing (optional)

1. Heat a medium-sized nonstick skillet over medium-high heat.

2. Crack the eggs into a mixing bowl. Add ¼ teaspoon of salt and beat with a fork until well blended.

3. Pour 2 tablespoons of the oil into the pan, then pour in the beaten eggs. Using a rubber spatula, move the eggs quickly from the outside in.

4. Once the base has started to cook but the surface still looks glossy, add the salmon and cheese and fold the base over the fillings, being careful not to overcook the eggs (you are aiming for a smooth, silky exterior with a pale color, not brown and crispy eggs). Transfer the omelette to a serving plate.

5. Put the watercress in a small bowl. Add the remaining 1 tablespoon of oil and a pinch of salt; toss well. Place the watercress on top of the omelette and garnish with more smoked salmon strips, if desired. Finish with pepper and Maldon salt, if using. Serve immediately.

Nutrition:		
Carb	Fat	Protein
3.9g	29g	46g

EGGS IN SPICED TOMATOES

SERVES 1

This breakfast dish is inspired by shakshuka, a well-loved North African classic. To make the recipe appropriate for Phase 1, the amount of tomatoes needs to be kept low, but that means the irresistible flavor explosion of shakshuka that you know and love is even more concentrated here. For Phases 2 and 3, you can add more diced tomatoes and even tomato puree to make the dish saucier and closer to the traditional shakshuka, where the eggs are poached in the gently simmering sauce. You can then serve it with a low-carb tortilla, pita bread, or another type of bread for sopping up the juices.

2 tablespoons olive oil

0.7 ounce (20g) sliced white onion

Salt and fresh ground black pepper

½ teaspoon smoked paprika

1 tablespoon thinly sliced jalapeño or other green chili pepper, plus more for garnish if desired (optional)

½ cup (120g) canned diced tomatoes with juice

⅔ cup (30g) fresh spinach, roughly chopped

2 large eggs

⅓ cup (50g) crumbled feta cheese

1. Heat the oil in a small skillet over low heat. Cook the onion with a small pinch each of salt and pepper until tender, 5 to 7 minutes.

2. Add the paprika and jalapeño, if using, and cook for 2 minutes, then add the tomatoes and cook for an additional 5 minutes.

3. Add the spinach and wilt down, cooking until any excess moisture has evaporated.

4. Make 2 wells for the eggs and crack an egg into the center of each well. Cover the pan and cook over low heat until the egg whites are set and the yolks are cooked to your liking, 5 to 8 minutes.

5. Scatter the feta over the top and season with a few good twists of pepper. If desired, garnish with jalapeño slices. Serve directly from the pan (use a trivet to protect your table), or transfer it to a plate if you prefer.

Nutrition:		
Carb	Fat	Protein
10.5g	22.7g	23.5g

BREAKFAST EGG BITES

MAKES
12 egg bites
(2 to 3 servings)

These egg bites are a fun change of pace when you're tired of scrambled eggs, or when you need a grab-and-go breakfast or snack in a hurry. Make multiple batches to keep on hand in the fridge for just this purpose. These are equally good eaten warm or cold, and they're perfect for including in a child's lunchbox. They're also infinitely customizable: use a different kind of semi-hard cheese if you like (smoked Gouda would be excellent), and consider using chopped pepperoni or diced ham instead of bacon.

1 tablespoon olive oil

6 large eggs

Salt and fresh ground black pepper

½ cup (50g) shredded cheddar cheese

½ cup (50g) crumbled or chopped cooked bacon

1. Preheat the oven to 350°F (180°C) and grease 12 wells of a standard-size muffin tin with the oil.

2. Whisk the eggs with a generous pinch each of salt and pepper. Divide the eggs between the prepared muffin wells, filling each about two-thirds full. (The egg bites will rise as they bake.) Stir in the cheese and bacon.

3. Bake until puffed and evenly browned on top, 15 to 18 minutes.

4. Remove the muffin tin from the oven and allow the egg bites to cool enough to touch before running a butter knife or small rubber spatula along the outer edge of each egg bite to release them.

5. Serve immediately, refrigerate for up to 3 days, or freeze for up to 3 months. To reheat the egg bites, simply place on a plate and microwave for 30 seconds or pop in a 350°F (180°C) oven for 5 minutes, until warmed through.

Nutrition per egg bite:		
Carb	Fat	Protein
0.6g	6.7g	6.7g

BROCCOLI AND FETA FRITTATA

SERVES 1

Eggs, cheese, and a nonstarchy vegetable—what could be more perfect for keto? This dish is quick, easy, and versatile. Change up the flavor by swapping in blue cheese or any other cheese for the feta. You can use just about any precooked nonstarchy vegetable here, too: spinach, kale, mushrooms, grilled onions, bell peppers, or asparagus. This is the ideal way to use up small bits of leftover veggies!

3 large eggs

Salt and fresh ground black pepper

1 tablespoon unsalted butter

1 cup (50g) roughly chopped broccoli florets, steamed or blanched

½ cup (50g) diced feta cheese

1. Preheat the oven to 350°F (180°C).

2. Heat a medium-sized oven-safe nonstick skillet over medium-high heat.

3. Crack the eggs into a bowl, season with a pinch each of salt and pepper, and whisk until combined.

4. When the skillet is hot (but not smoking), put the butter in the pan and let it foam. Tilt the skillet back and forth to cover the bottom with the melted butter.

5. Add the eggs, sprinkle the broccoli and feta over the eggs, and put the skillet in the oven. Bake until the eggs are firm and golden brown, 5 to 10 minutes.

6. Sprinkle with a pinch of pepper. Serve the frittata directly from the skillet (use a trivet to protect your table) or gently slide it onto a serving plate.

Nutrition:		
Carb	Fat	Protein
8g	27g	27.3g

APPETIZERS AND SNACKS

Just because you're watching your carb intake doesn't mean snacking is off-limits. Sure, pretzels, granola bars, and chocolate candies are mostly off the menu, but there's a world of other things you can reach for when you need something small to tide you over between meals. And remember, when your blood sugar is well controlled from eating low-carb or keto, you won't need to snack much. Your appetite will be reduced provided you're eating substantial enough portions at mealtime. So often we snack on autopilot, out of pure habit, or because others around us are eating rather than because we are genuinely hungry.

It's totally fine if you do find yourself wanting to reach for snacks, though. It can be hard to break the habit after a lifetime of doing it! I hope you'll feel excited to try the snack recipes in this chapter, but here are some suggestions for simple keto or low-carb options to keep on hand when a snack attack hits:

- Beef jerky or biltong (low- or no-sugar)
- Berries or other fruits (Phases 2 and 3)
- Boiled eggs
- Canned seafood (tuna, salmon, mackerel, sardines)
- Cheeses
- Cold cooked shrimp
- Cold cuts (low-sugar) (roast beef, pastrami, roasted turkey, roasted chicken breast)
- Cooked bacon
- Cooked sausages
- Cucumber slices
- Cured meats (pepperoni, salami, prosciutto)
- Deviled eggs
- Grilled chicken breast tenderloins
- Grilled steak, sliced
- Jicama sticks
- Marinated mushrooms or artichokes
- Nuts and seeds
- Olives
- Pickles or gherkins
- Pork rinds

Beef and Zucchini Frikkadels / **54**

Crispy Chicken Wings / **56**

Two-Minute Cheese and Chive Rolls / **58**

Marinated Feta Cheese / **60**

Pan-Seared Halloumi / **62**

Dressed Olives / **64**

Toasted Sesame Cabbage Snacks / **66**

Kale Chips / **68**

BEEF AND ZUCCHINI FRIKKADELS

SERVES 4

Frikkadels are South African meatballs. To make them keto-friendly, I've swapped out the traditional breadcrumbs for zucchini to make sure they stay moist. These little nuggets are so versatile. You can eat them while they're warm or have them chilled as a snack. (They're incredibly popular that way in South Africa.) They're also a good match for Roasted Tomato Sauce (page 218) served with zucchini noodles. They freeze well, too, so consider making a big batch and stashing some away for later. Get creative with the spices. Coriander is traditional for frikkadels, but use whatever spice(s) you like.

1 medium-large zucchini (about 7 ounces/200g)

1 pound (500g) ground beef

1 large egg, lightly beaten

1 teaspoon ground coriander

3 cloves garlic, grated

Salt, plain or flavored (see page 271)

Fresh ground black pepper

Maldon salt, for finishing (optional)

1. Preheat the oven to 400°F (200°C). Line a rimmed baking sheet with parchment paper.

2. Grate the zucchini and place it in the center of a clean tea towel. Gather both ends of the towel and wring out the excess moisture. Put the zucchini in a large bowl.

3. Add the ground beef, egg, coriander, and garlic to the bowl, season with a pinch each of salt and pepper, and mix well with your hands.

4. Roll the meat mixture into 2-inch (5cm) balls and place them on the prepared baking sheet. (You should end up with about 20 meatballs.) Bake until the meatballs are nicely browned and the juices run clear when pierced with the tip of a knife, 15 to 20 minutes.

5. Sprinkle a pinch of Maldon salt on top, if desired. Serve right away or chill the meatballs in the fridge and enjoy them cold. They will keep well for up to 3 days in the fridge or up to 3 months in the freezer.

Nutrition per serving:		
Carb	Fat	Protein
3.3g	12.3g	30g

CRISPY CHICKEN WINGS

SERVES 3

Chicken wings are one of my go-to appetizers when I have a few mates over to watch rugby; they work wonderfully as a snack. You don't have to eat keto or low-carb to love wings, especially when they're this crispy. This recipe is foolproof and will give you extra-crispy wings every time. Plan ahead, though: for the best results, you'll want to let the seasoned wings dry in the fridge overnight before you cook them. It's an extra step, but trust me, it's worth it. The drier the wings, the crispier they'll get.

WINGS:

1 teaspoon smoked paprika

1 teaspoon baking powder

Salt and fresh ground black pepper

1 pound (500g) chicken wings

GLAZE:

3½ tablespoons (50g) unsalted butter

1 clove garlic, crushed to a paste or minced

1 tablespoon red wine vinegar

2 teaspoons cayenne pepper

1 teaspoon salt

½ teaspoon fresh ground black pepper

Chopped fresh cilantro, parsley, chives, or other herb, for garnish (optional)

Blue Cheese Dip (page 202), for serving (optional)

1. Prepare the wings: Mix together the paprika, baking powder, and a pinch each of salt and pepper. Coat the wings thoroughly with the mixture and arrange them, skin side up, in a single layer on a rimmed baking sheet, leaving space between them. Put the baking sheet in the fridge to let the wings dry overnight.

2. When you're ready to cook the wings, preheat the oven to 400°F (200°C).

3. Remove the baking sheet from the fridge and put it in the oven. Bake the wings until golden brown, 30 to 40 minutes.

4. Meanwhile, make the glaze: Heat the butter and garlic in a small saucepan over medium-high heat until the butter is fully melted. Remove from the heat and whisk in the vinegar and cayenne.

5. When the wings are done and while they're still hot, transfer them to a large bowl. Use a rubber spatula to scrape every bit of the glaze from the saucepan into the bowl. Toss the wings until they are thoroughly coated with the glaze. Season with the salt and pepper. Serve immediately, garnished with the fresh herb of your choice and with blue cheese dip on the side, if desired.

Nutrition per serving:		
Carb	Fat	Protein
0.9g	26.8g	50.8g

TWO-MINUTE CHEESE AND CHIVE ROLLS

MAKES
2 rolls (1 per serving)

Homemade low-carb rolls that take only two minutes to make? Yes! Don't let the long list of ingredients intimidate you. This is a simple and fast way to make a bread replacement. These rolls are very versatile; not only do they make a perfect snack, but they are also great with a soup, salad, or main dish. So consider making a large batch, especially since they freeze beautifully for up to three months and take less than a minute to warm up in the microwave.

---

2 large eggs

2 tablespoons whole milk or half-and-half

1½ tablespoons olive oil, plus more for greasing the ramekins

⅓ cup (30g) blanched almond flour

⅓ cup (30g) coconut flour

½ teaspoon baking powder

Salt and fresh ground black pepper

¼ cup (30g) shredded cheddar cheese

2 tablespoons chopped fresh chives

1. In a large bowl, whisk together the eggs, milk, and oil until well combined.

2. Sift the flours and baking powder into a medium-sized bowl and season with a pinch each of salt and pepper. Whisk to combine, then stir in the wet ingredients. Fold in the cheese and chives.

3. Lightly grease two 4-ounce (60ml) ramekins and divide the mixture between them. Set a kitchen towel on the counter and gently tap the ramekins on it to get rid of air pockets (you want your rolls to have a tight crumb without any holes).

4. Microwave both ramekins at the same time on high for 90 seconds. Turn the rolls out onto a cutting board or plate, let them cool for a minute, and then slice them in half horizontally.

5. Enjoy the rolls plain or toast them in a toaster oven or under the broiler for a few minutes. You can also pan-fry them in a small amount of oil or melted butter until golden brown, as pictured.

Nutrition per serving:		
Carb	Fat	Protein
5.5g	34.9g	14.7g

MARINATED FETA CHEESE

SERVES 6

I always have a tub of this marinated feta in the fridge at home. My family loves it on just about everything. The low carb and high protein content make it a guilt-free addition. You can spread it on low-carb crackers or pizza, top a salad with it, or enjoy it as a simple snack. (For those following Phase 2 or 3, the marinated cheese is dynamite with sliced peaches or cubed watermelon.) This simple recipe is tasty as-is, but feel free to spice it up a bit with pesto or harissa, a North African chili paste that can be found at many supermarkets. And if you have some marinade left over after all the cheese cubes are gone, save it! You can use it to add saltiness and tang to so many things—without adding too many carbs.

---

7 ounces (200g) feta cheese in brine

8 tablespoons olive oil, divided

2 cloves garlic, thinly sliced

3.5 ounces (100g) ripe tomatoes, seeded and finely chopped

Salt and fresh ground black pepper

1 ounce (30g) fresh basil leaves, roughly chopped

1 tablespoon white wine vinegar

1. Remove the feta from the brine and cut it into large cubes or chunks. Set aside.

2. Put 2 tablespoons of the oil and the garlic in a medium-sized skillet over medium heat. Cook, stirring often, until the garlic is tender, about 4 minutes (watch closely—garlic burns quickly).

3. Add the tomatoes and season with a pinch each of salt and pepper. Cook until the tomatoes have broken down, about 6 minutes.

4. Add the basil and cook for another 2 minutes, then remove from the heat and adjust the seasoning to your liking.

5. Add the remaining 6 tablespoons of oil, the vinegar, and the feta; toss gently until the feta is well covered with the tomatoes. Transfer to a container and refrigerate for at least 12 hours before serving to give the feta time to absorb the flavors. It will keep in the fridge for up to a week.

Nutrition per serving:		
Carb	Fat	Protein
1.1g	15.7g	5.6g

PHASE 1

PAN-SEARED HALLOUMI

SERVES 2

This recipe is quick and easy to put together, very low in carbs, and packed with protein. Oh, and it's delicious—what more could a low-carber want? Halloumi is a Greek cheese that, owing to its low acidity and the strength of its protein matrix, doesn't melt when it's cooked, so it's great for grilling or pan-frying. Grilled halloumi is often offered as an appetizer in Greek restaurants.

10.5 ounces (300g) halloumi cheese

1 tablespoon olive oil

Salt, plain or flavored (see page 271)

Fresh ground black pepper

3 tablespoons lemon juice

1. Heat a large nonstick skillet over high heat.

2. Cut the cheese into 2-inch (5cm) batons; place in a small bowl. Add the oil and toss to coat. Season lightly with salt and pepper.

3. Cook the cheese in the skillet until golden brown and crispy on all sides, about 1 minute per side. Remove from the skillet and finish with the lemon juice.

Nutrition per serving:		
Carb	Fat	Protein
1.5g	44.5g	33g

DRESSED OLIVES

SERVES 2

The first time I tasted a dressed olive, I was working at Hibiscus, a two Michelin-starred restaurant in London, under the renowned French chef Claude Bosi. I had been in kitchens for years, and it had never crossed my mind to add more flavor to an already tasty little morsel of food. Once I tasted one, though, I realized I had been missing out! Not only are dressed olives delicious, but they're insanely easy to make. Consider making an extra-large batch for your next cocktail party.

The possibilities are endless with this recipe, from the olive varieties you use to the flavors you impart to them. Olives are like wine: everyone has their favorites. Mine is the bright green and fleshy Nocellara from Sicily. These olives, also labeled Castelvetrano olives, are staples in Italian specialty shops, but you can find them at many supermarkets as well. Use whichever olives you prefer, although green ones look best here. (And make sure the ones you use aren't stuffed with something that won't jibe with the recipe.)

2 cups (300g) Nocellara olives or other olives of choice

2 tablespoons extra-virgin olive oil

Grated zest and juice of ½ lemon

1 tablespoon finely chopped fresh chives

1 tablespoon finely chopped fresh parsley

Salt and fresh ground black pepper

Maldon salt, for finishing (optional)

Combine all the ingredients except the salt and pepper in a bowl large enough to toss them together well. Season lightly with salt and pepper to taste. They can be served immediately (with a pinch of Maldon salt as a finishing touch, if desired) or stored in the fridge for the flavors to meld. Note that good olive oil congeals or solidifies in the fridge, so if you chill your olives, take them out of the fridge a few minutes before serving so the oil will return to the proper texture.

I told you it was easy!

Nutrition per serving:		
Carb	Fat	Protein
8.3g	48.1g	1.9g

PHASE ①

TOASTED SESAME CABBAGE SNACKS

SERVES 4

I stumbled across this simple yet delicious snack while traveling through Japan. Talk about an international experience: I can't think of a bar anywhere else in the world that would serve cabbage to snack on! That's a shame, because once I mustered the courage to try this recipe, I was astounded at how good it was, and now I often serve it to guests as a pre-dinner snack. With just three ingredients and a very small amount of carbohydrate, it just might become one of your go-to bites.

½ small head green cabbage (about 8 ounces/250g)

2 tablespoons toasted sesame oil

Maldon salt

Toasted sesame seeds (white and/or black), for garnish (optional)

1. Cut the half head of cabbage lengthwise into quarters. Remove the core and separate the cabbage into strips.

2. Wash the cabbage strips in ice-cold water (this will help keep them very crunchy). Drain well, shake off the excess moisture, and put the strips in a large bowl.

3. Drizzle the cabbage with the oil and toss to coat well. Season with a healthy pinch of Maldon salt (be sure to drizzle the oil on first; otherwise, the salt will fall right off). If desired, sprinkle lightly with toasted sesame seeds for extra crunch and visual interest. Serve immediately, as the cabbage will soften quickly.

Nutrition per serving:		
Carb	Fat	Protein
1.8g	3.5g	0.6g

KALE CHIPS

SERVES 1

Who doesn't love chips, right? But on a low-carb diet, especially when you're in Phase 1, potatoes and corn are out, so no potato chips or tortilla chips. Pork rinds are a great stand-in when you need something crunchy and salty, but it never hurts to have another option up your sleeve, whether it's because you simply want to change things up now and then or you're entertaining guests who avoid pork. If you claim to dislike kale, I challenge you to give these chips a try. I understand that not everyone's a fan of raw kale in salads, but I predict you'll have a hard time keeping your hands out of a crispy batch of these chips. In fact, prepare a second batch while you're eating the first—you're going to want it!

3.5 ounces (100g) stemmed kale, washed and spun dry

1 tablespoon olive oil, avocado oil, or melted coconut oil

1 teaspoon Super Seasoning Blend (page 272) or other flavored salt, such as garlic salt

Mayonnaise, homemade (page 208) or store-bought, for serving (optional)

1. Preheat the oven to 350°F (180°C).

2. Cut the kale leaves into chip-sized pieces (keep some larger pieces if you like) and place them in a large bowl. Add the oil and toss to coat, then add the seasoning and toss again.

3. Arrange the kale in a single layer on a rimmed baking sheet and bake until the leaves are crispy and the edges are lightly charred, about 10 minutes. Let cool completely before serving.

4. Serve with mayonnaise, if desired.

Nutrition:		
Carb	Fat	Protein
4.4g	15.5g	2.9g

SALADS AND SOUPS

People who don't know much about ketogenic and low-carb diets often have the false impression that you eat nothing but bunless bacon cheeseburgers and rib-eye steaks covered in melted butter—with a side of extra butter! While that sounds decadent and delicious, the truth is, one thing and one thing only makes a keto diet effective, and that's keeping carbs low. With that in mind, there's a world of possibilities for colorful salads that are light and tasty, crunchy and vibrant—and some are even substantial enough to be a meal. Soups are also easy to keep low-carb when you thicken them with cream or pureed vegetables.

To increase the carbohydrate quantity or ingredient variety for Phase 2, these soups and salads can be served with low-carb crackers or cheese crisps. (Some people even use pork rinds as croutons!) You can also sprinkle toasted nuts or seeds on a salad where appropriate. For Phase 3, the soups and salads can be served with your preferred bread. A crusty baguette is always a sure thing with soup.

Warm Kale and Blue Cheese Salad with Walnuts and Bacon **/ 72**

Bacon-y Caesar Salad **/ 74**

Tomato Salad with Burrata, Herbs, and Poppy Seeds **/ 76**

Goat Cheese, Red Cabbage, Green Bean, and Almond Salad **/ 78**

Chargrilled Zucchini with Crispy Halloumi and Kale Pesto **/ 80**

Barley Salad with Marinated Feta, Peas, and Mint **/ 82**

Orange, Celery, and Fennel Salad with Blue Cheese and
Pumpkin Seeds **/ 84**

Broccoli, Spinach, and Stilton Soup **/ 86**

Cauliflower Cheese and Pancetta Soup **/ 88**

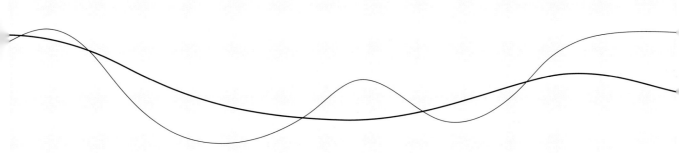

WARM KALE AND BLUE CHEESE SALAD WITH WALNUTS AND BACON

SERVES 1

You can't beat the combination of tangy blue cheese, crisp bacon, bright vinegar, and earthy kale, which helps balance things nicely. You can turn this salad into a complete meal by adding grilled chicken or steak, either of which would be dynamite with these flavors.

3.5 ounces (100g) bacon, cut into 1-inch (2.5cm) pieces

7 raw walnuts, roughly chopped

1 tablespoon unsalted butter

3.5 ounces (100g) stemmed and chopped kale

Salt and fresh ground black pepper

¼ cup (50g) crumbled blue cheese

DRESSING:

2 tablespoons extra-virgin olive oil

1 teaspoon whole-grain mustard

1 tablespoon red wine vinegar

1. Cook the bacon pieces over medium-high heat in a skillet large enough to accommodate the kale. Once the bacon is crispy, transfer it to a paper towel–lined plate and leave the skillet with the bacon fat in it on the burner. Add the chopped walnuts and cook, stirring often, for 1 minute. Transfer the walnuts to the bacon plate, leaving the bacon fat in the pan and keeping the burner on high. Add the butter.

2. Add the kale and cook until wilted and tender with a slight bite, 2 to 3 minutes; season lightly with salt and pepper to taste. (Go easy on the salt at first; the bacon and blue cheese will provide additional salt.) Transfer to a medium-sized bowl.

3. Add the prepared bacon and walnuts to the kale and mix to distribute evenly.

4. Make the dressing: Whisk together the oil, mustard, and vinegar until combined. Add to the kale and mix to coat evenly.

5. Transfer the salad to a serving plate. Top with the blue cheese and enjoy.

FOR PHASE 2: *Add cubed and roasted beets or butternut squash. These vegetables fit seamlessly with kale.*

FOR PHASE 3: *Add a small scoop of a cooked grain, such as quinoa or farro, or cooked beans.*

Nutrition:		
Carb	Fat	Protein
10.9g	84.6g	59.3g

BACON-Y CAESAR SALAD

SERVES 1

This salad is the perfect combination of flavors and textures. It's got umami from the Parmesan cheese, anchovies, and bacon; it's salty and tangy; it's creamy; and the lettuce keeps things cool and crisp. You could serve this alongside grilled chicken or beef to make a complete meal, or simply keep it as a traditional salad. It also makes an eye-catching appetizer if you fill individual gem or endive leaves with the ingredients.

I use fresh anchovy fillets marinated in oil, which come vacuum-packed and can be found in the seafood section of many grocery stores. If you can't find them, you can use salt-cured anchovy fillets in oil, which come in rectangular flat cans or glass jars. However, be sure to rinse them under cold running water first, as they are quite salty.

7 ounces (200g) baby gem lettuce, Belgian endive, romaine, or butter lettuce

1.4 ounces (40g) bacon, cooked and roughly chopped

2 ounces (50g) marinated anchovy fillets

1½ tablespoons shaved Parmesan cheese

2 tablespoons Simple Salad Dressing (page 212)

Fresh ground black pepper

1. If using baby gem lettuce or Belgian endive, cut each head lengthwise into wedges. If using romaine or butter lettuce, separate several individual leaves and tear into bite-sized pieces. Arrange the lettuce on a plate.

2. Layer the bacon, anchovies, and Parmesan in between the leaves or layers of lettuce.

3. Drizzle with the dressing and season with pepper to taste.

Nutrition:		
Carb	Fat	Protein
11.8g	75.2g	67.5g

TOMATO SALAD WITH BURRATA, HERBS, AND POPPY SEEDS

SERVES 1

Burrata is one of my favorite cheeses, and this is a great way to feature it. Burrata is an Italian cheese, typically made from cow's milk, comprising mozzarella and cream. A ball of burrata is shaped like a round drawstring purse, with the outside having the texture of fresh mozzarella and the inside being soft and creamy—what's not to love about that? Here, burrata pairs perfectly with the acidity and sweetness of the tomatoes and the crunch from the poppy seeds. Most supermarkets with good cheese selections carry burrata, but if you can't find it, fresh mozzarella will work just as well. Maldon salt is a must in this recipe! The crunchy flakes add a nice textural contrast to the creamy burrata.

10.5 ounces (300g) heirloom cherry tomatoes

1 tablespoon red wine vinegar

4 tablespoons extra-virgin olive oil, divided

Maldon salt and fresh ground black pepper

9 fresh basil leaves

9 fresh parsley leaves

3.5 ounces (100g) burrata

1 teaspoon poppy seeds or black sesame seeds

1. Slice the tomatoes crosswise into rounds, ¼ to ⅓ inch (6 to 8mm) thick; layer them on a serving plate. Drizzle on the vinegar and 3 tablespoons of the oil; season with Maldon salt and pepper to taste.

2. Tear the fresh herbs into pieces and scatter them over the tomatoes.

3. Place the cheese in the center and top with the poppy seeds, the remaining 1 tablespoon of oil, and a bit more salt and pepper. Serve immediately.

Nutrition:		
Carb	Fat	Protein
8.4g	70g	12.4g

GOAT CHEESE, RED CABBAGE, GREEN BEAN, AND ALMOND SALAD

SERVES 1

The bitterness of cabbage and the creaminess of goat cheese are a match made in heaven. I made a variation of this salad many years ago at the Grosvenor House Hotel, pairing pine nuts with arugula and sometimes chicory with almonds, so feel free to experiment with the ingredients as long as you keep in mind that the macros will be different from the numbers shown here. The amount of goat cheese I've called for packs enough protein to make this an entrée salad, so use less if you prefer it as a starter.

Salt

1 cup (150g) green beans, ends trimmed

½ cup (50g) thinly sliced red cabbage, divided

1 cup (50g) fresh spinach, divided

4 tablespoons Simple Salad Dressing (page 212), divided

Fresh ground black pepper

10 whole almonds

1 (7-ounce/200g) round or log soft-ripened goat cheese with rind

Olive oil, for brushing

1. Set an oven rack about 10 inches (25cm) away from the heating elements. Preheat the broiler to 425°F (220°C). Line a rimmed baking sheet with parchment paper.

2. Fill a medium-sized saucepan with water and bring to a rapid boil over high heat. Add a large pinch of salt and the green beans; cook until tender, 5 to 8 minutes. Drain and put the beans in a medium-sized bowl.

3. While the green beans are cooking, put half of the cabbage and half of the spinach in a medium-sized mixing bowl.

4. Drain the beans well and add them to the bowl with the cabbage and spinach. Add 3 tablespoons of the dressing and mix well. Season with salt and pepper to taste; set aside.

5. Toast the almonds in a medium-sized skillet over medium heat until fragrant, about 90 seconds (keep an eye on them; nuts can go from perfectly toasted to completely burned in a split second). Remove from the heat and transfer to a plate to cool.

6. If desired, reserve 2 almonds to grate over the salad and roughly chop the rest. Add the chopped almonds to the salad.

7. If using a cheese log, slice the cheese into thick rounds. Arrange the rounds in a single layer on the lined baking sheet. Brush lightly with olive oil and season with a pinch each of salt and pepper. Broil until the cheese just begins to melt, 3 to 5 minutes.

Nutrition:		
Carb	Fat	Protein
18.2g	44.7g	31.1g

8. Arrange the remaining cabbage and spinach on a serving plate and top with the warm salad, followed by the cheese. Drizzle with the remaining 1 tablespoon of dressing and, if you've reserved 2 almonds, grate them with a Microplane on top to garnish.

FOR PHASE 1: *Simply omit the almonds.*

CHARGRILLED ZUCCHINI WITH CRISPY HALLOUMI AND KALE PESTO

SERVES 1

Halloumi cheese is incredibly versatile (see Pan-Seared Halloumi, page 62). It originated in Cyprus and is traditionally made from goat's milk or sheep's milk but may also be made from cow's milk. It's packed with protein and, owing to its molecular structure, the cheese holds together when cooked and doesn't melt. Because of this, halloumi is sometimes used as a meat substitute in vegetarian dishes. It's best to use a grill pan here, which will impart those lovely grill marks to the cheese.

1 small zucchini (about 3.5 ounces/100g)

3 tablespoons olive oil, divided

Salt and fresh ground black pepper

½ cup (100g) cherry tomatoes, quartered

½ cup (10g) arugula

3 tablespoons kale pesto, homemade (page 214) or store-bought, divided

7 ounces (200g) halloumi cheese

Maldon salt, for finishing (optional)

1. Preheat a grill pan (or a small skillet) over high heat.

2. Cut the zucchini lengthwise into 6 spears and put them in a small bowl. Add 1 tablespoon of the oil and toss to coat.

3. Season the zucchini spears with a pinch each of salt and pepper and char them on all sides to get some grill marks (or a good sear, if using a skillet), about 2 minutes. Return them to the bowl. Keep the grill pan on the heat.

4. Add the tomatoes, arugula, 1 tablespoon of the oil, and about one-quarter of the pesto to the charred zucchini; mix well and set aside.

5. Cut the halloumi cheese into 3 thick slices. Lightly coat with the remaining 1 tablespoon of oil and season with a pinch each of salt and pepper. In the same hot grill pan, char the cheese on both sides, about 1 minute per side. (Be sure that your pan is very hot, or the cheese will stick.)

6. To serve, spread the remaining pesto on a serving plate, arrange the dressed vegetables on the pesto, and lay the cheese on top. Finish with Maldon salt and more pepper, if desired.

Nutrition:		
Carb	Fat	Protein
10.4g	75.4g	50.8g

BARLEY SALAD WITH MARINATED FETA, PEAS, AND MINT

SERVES 1

This hearty salad is packed with texture and taste. This recipe makes one serving, but you can easily double or triple it to serve more. I recommend that you use frozen peas; being picked at peak ripeness, they're wonderfully and consistently sweet. In fact, I'll let you in on a little secret—in every Michelin-starred restaurant I've worked in, we almost always used frozen peas. If it's good enough for the premier leagues, it's good enough for me!

Salt

1 cup (80g) sugar snap peas

⅓ cup (50g) frozen peas

⅓ cup (100g) pearl barley

10 fresh mint leaves, divided

2 ounces (50g) radishes, thinly sliced with a knife or shaved with a mandoline

3 tablespoons marinade from Marinated Feta Cheese (page 60), divided

Fresh ground black pepper

3.5 ounces (100g) feta cubes from Marinated Feta Cheese (page 60)

1. Keep a bowl of ice water near the stove. Fill a medium-sized pot with about 2 quarts (2 liters) of water and bring to a rapid boil over high heat. Stir in ½ teaspoon of salt and blanch the sugar snap peas until tender, 3 to 5 minutes; immediately transfer the sugar snap peas to the ice water with a fine-mesh strainer or slotted spoon to refresh. Keep the water boiling.

2. Add the frozen peas to the boiling water and blanch for 90 seconds, then transfer them to the bowl of ice water with the sugar snap peas. Continue to keep the water boiling.

3. Add the pearl barley to the boiling water and lower the heat to a gentle simmer; cook, uncovered, until tender, 25 to 30 minutes. Drain and transfer to a medium-sized bowl.

4. Drain the sugar snap peas and peas and add them to the bowl with the cooked barley. Finely chop 5 of the mint leaves and add them to the bowl along with the radishes.

5. Stir in 2 tablespoons of the feta marinade and season to taste with salt and pepper. Spoon the mixture onto a serving plate and arrange the feta cubes on top. Drizzle with the remaining 1 tablespoon of marinade and garnish with the remaining 5 mint leaves, roughly torn, and some fresh ground pepper.

Nutrition:		
Carb	Fat	Protein
48.4g	91.6g	24.6g

ORANGE, CELERY, AND FENNEL SALAD WITH BLUE CHEESE AND PUMPKIN SEEDS

SERVES 1

This salad is incredibly refreshing and a great palate cleanser in the summer. The key is to slice the vegetables as finely as possible; otherwise, you'll spend half the day chewing and feel like you've turned into a rabbit!

---

2 stalks celery

5.3 ounces (150g) trimmed fennel bulb

1 navel orange

2 tablespoons Simple Salad Dressing (page 212)

Salt and fresh ground black pepper

2 ounces (50g) crumbled blue cheese

1 tablespoon toasted pumpkin seeds (see Note)

1. Using a sharp knife or a mandoline, finely slice the celery and fennel and place in a bowl of ice water. (This will keep them crisp.)

2. Use a sharp knife to slice off the top and bottom of the orange. Remove the skin and the pith by slicing downward following the curvature of the fruit, being careful not to trim away too much of the segments. Cut between the connective membranes to release the segments into a small bowl and set aside. Squeeze every bit of the juice remaining in the membranes into a separate medium-sized bowl.

3. Put the dressing in the bowl with the orange juice and stir to combine. Adjust the seasoning to taste with salt and pepper.

4. Drain the shaved vegetables and pat them dry with a clean kitchen towel. Add them to the bowl with the dressing and toss well.

5. Place the salad on a plate and scatter the orange segments, blue cheese, and pumpkin seeds on top.

Nutrition:		
Carb	Fat	Protein
29.6g	14.8g	19.9g

NOTE: *If you have raw pumpkin seeds on hand, toast them in a small skillet over medium heat for about 90 seconds. They will almost pop like popcorn.*

BROCCOLI, SPINACH, AND STILTON SOUP

SERVES 4

This soup is a British classic that also happens to be quick to prepare and perfect for keto diets. If you're not a fan of blue cheese, try ricotta, feta, or goat cheese. I add some spinach at the end to give the soup an even more vibrant color—not to mention extra nutrients, like folate, vitamin K, and beta-carotene.

3 tablespoons olive oil, plus more for drizzling

1 cup (100g) finely chopped celery

Salt and fresh ground black pepper

1 quart (1 liter) chicken broth, homemade (page 264) or store-bought

10 cups (500g) chopped broccoli crowns or florets

3½ tablespoons (50g) unsalted butter

1½ cups (75g) fresh spinach

3.5 ounces (100g) Stilton cheese or any type of blue cheese, crumbled

1. Heat the oil in a large deep saucepan over medium-low heat. Add the celery, a pinch of salt, and a touch of pepper. Sweat the celery with a lid on (you don't want it to brown) until tender, 5 to 10 minutes. Remove the lid, then add the broth and another pinch of salt, raise the heat, and bring to a boil.

2. Once at a rapid boil, add the broccoli and cook, uncovered, until the broccoli is tender, 10 to 15 minutes.

3. Remove the pan from the heat and stir in the butter and spinach. Transfer to a blender in batches and blend until smooth. Use caution when blending hot liquids! (You can use an immersion blender, but it may not get the soup quite as smooth and silky.)

4. Adjust the seasoning with more salt and pepper if needed. Serve hot topped with the cheese. Drizzle each bowl with about 1 teaspoon olive oil and finish with a pinch of pepper.

NOTE: *If you're making this soup ahead of time to serve later or another day, I recommend that you bring the temperature down as rapidly as possible after step 3, before refrigerating the soup in an airtight container. Rapid cooling is an extra step, but it's effective for preserving the soup's beautiful green color. To cool the soup, fill your kitchen sink or a large bowl half or two-thirds full with ice and cold water, position the saucepan in the ice bath to be level with the ice, and stir occasionally to help release the heat and cool the soup evenly. (Alternatively, if you have a large freezer, you can spread the hot soup in a thin layer on a rimmed baking sheet and place it in the freezer until the soup is ice cold but not frozen.) To reheat, simply place the desired amount in a saucepan, set over medium-high heat, and stir until the soup starts to boil, then remove and serve immediately.*

Nutrition per serving:		
Carb	Fat	Protein
10g	32.3g	12.7g

FOR PHASE 2 OR PHASE 3: *Serve the soup with low-carb crackers, croutons, or a slice of crusty baguette.*

CAULIFLOWER CHEESE AND PANCETTA SOUP

SERVES 4

Cauliflower has become quite a workhorse in the low-carb world. It's a nonstarchy stand-in for mashed potatoes, rice, macaroni and cheese, and even potato salad. Just as in some of those dishes, cauliflower serves as the blank canvas in this wonderfully warming winter soup, allowing the beautiful palette of flavors—and textures—of the pancetta and cheese to shine.

1½ tablespoons unsalted butter

1 pound (500g) cauliflower, roughly chopped

Salt and fresh ground black pepper

2 cups (480ml) chicken broth, homemade (page 264) or store-bought, or water

1 cup (240ml) heavy cream

7 ounces (200g) diced pancetta or thick-sliced bacon, cut crosswise into lardons

½ cup (50g) grated Parmesan cheese

Finely chopped chives, for garnish (optional)

1. Melt the butter in a large saucepan over low heat. Add the cauliflower and a pinch each of salt and pepper. (Go easy on the salt here; a small pinch will do, as the bacon and cheese will add more salt.) Cover with a lid and sweat it down until it softens, 5 to 10 minutes, ensuring the cauliflower doesn't brown.

2. Pour in the broth and cream and bring to a gentle simmer. Cook, covered, until the cauliflower is fork-tender, 8 to 12 minutes.

3. While the soup is simmering, cook the pancetta in a small skillet over medium heat, stirring often, until crisp, 4 to 5 minutes. Transfer the pancetta to a paper towel–lined plate and scrape the rendered fat in the skillet into a small bowl; set both aside.

4. Once the soup is ready, stir in the Parmesan. Transfer to a blender in batches and blend until smooth. Use caution when blending hot liquids! (You can use an immersion blender, but it may not get the soup quite as smooth and silky.)

5. Adjust the seasoning with more salt and pepper if needed. Divide among 4 bowls, top with the crispy pancetta along with some of the reserved pancetta fat, and finish with a pinch of pepper. If desired, garnish with chives.

Nutrition per serving:		
Carb	Fat	Protein
9.4g	67g	16.5g

FOR PHASE 2 OR PHASE 3: *Serve the soup with low-carb crackers, croutons, or a slice of crusty baguette.*

MAIN DISHES

Hearty main dishes are the mainstays of a low-carb diet. You can eat your fill of protein foods and the fats that come with them and round things out with nonstarchy vegetable sides if you like. Protein and fat have very different effects on your body's hunger and fullness signals compared to carbohydrates, especially refined carbs. The dishes in this chapter will help keep you satiated so you don't find yourself reaching for a snack a short while later, as you were probably accustomed to doing in your higher-carb past. When you're putting a meal together, the sky's the limit—beef, lamb, pork, chicken, seafood, or eggs. Just keep the carbs where they need to be for the phase you're following.

Some of these recipes are complete meals all on their own. For those that are best paired with a side dish, choose recipes from this book, or use whatever nonstarchy vegetables you like for Phase 1. For Phase 2 or 3, simply adjust as appropriate for your carbohydrate tolerance. For Phase 2, it might be as simple as adding a Phase 2 vegetable, such as beets, carrots, or winter squash. For Phase 3, add a scoop of cooked rice (or another type of grain), a baked potato, or a serving of pasta. (Consider cooking large quantities of these starchy sides ahead of time to have on hand for the higher-carb eaters in your household.) You could also add beans or other legumes where they fit nicely with a particular recipe, or a hunk of crusty bread.

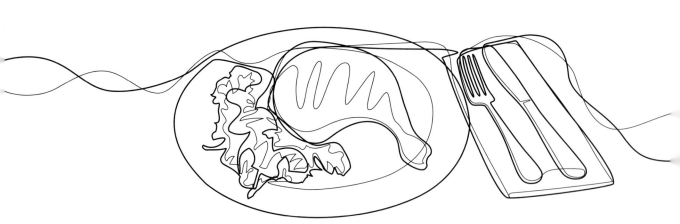

Stuffed Roasted Zucchini with Tomato and Herb Salsa / **92**

Foil-Wrapped Salmon with Cumin-Spiced Cauliflower Rice / **94**

Soy-Cured Salmon with Fennel and Cucumber Salad / **96**

Zoodle Carbonara / **98**

Dad's Singapore Zoodles / **100**

Pan-Fried NY Strip Steak with Charred Green Beans, Arugula, and Quick-Pickled Scallions / **104**

Beef Tacos in Lettuce Cups with Lime Crema / **106**

Black Pepper Chicken Ramen / **108**

Seared Tuna with Avocado, Cucumber, and Tomato Salad / **110**

Garlic Prawns / **112**

Crispy Chicken Leg Quarters with Sesame, Soy, and Leafy Greens / **114**

Pan-Seared Lamb Chops with Roasted Vegetables and Yogurt Mint Sauce / **116**

Kung Pao Chicken / **118**

Cottage Pie / **120**

Zucchini Lasagna / **124**

Moussaka / **126**

Peri-Peri Chicken / **130**

Pot-au-Feu / **132**

Bacon and Brie Burgers with Zesty Toppings / **134**

Smoked Haddock with Hollandaise and Fennel Butter Cabbage / **136**

Slow-Cooked Pork Ribs / **138**

Roasted Rosemary and Garlic Leg of Lamb / **140**

Asparagus with Prosciutto, Poached Egg, and Arugula / **142**

Calamari with Chorizo / **144**

Ruby Murray Chicken Curry / **146**

Zoodle Bolognese / **148**

Fish Pie / **150**

Mediterranean Trout with Crushed Peas and Tomato-Radish Salsa / **152**

Sea Bass with Lemon Butter and Mashed Broccoli / **154**

Five-Minute Salmon / **156**

Tortilla Pizza / **158**

Fish Carpaccio with Radish and Smashed Avocado / **160**

Pork Chops with Braised Cabbage and Mustard-Cheese Sauce / **162**

Spicy Meatballs in Roasted Tomato Sauce / **164**

Moules Marinières / **166**

Rosemary Baked Chicken with Green Beans and Tomatoes / **168**

STUFFED ROASTED ZUCCHINI WITH TOMATO AND HERB SALSA

SERVES 4

This dish is a sensory explosion. There's a nice contrast between the hot zucchini and the cool, refreshing labneh, and the vibrant, colorful salsa makes it exciting for the eyes, too. Labneh is a thick, creamy Middle Eastern yogurt cheese. It's available in any Middle Eastern grocery, but full-fat Greek yogurt or sour cream will work perfectly fine as a substitute.

6 very small zucchini (about 14 ounces/400g total)

4 tablespoons olive oil, divided

Salt and fresh ground black pepper

½ cup (50g) diced shallots or red onions

1 clove garlic, minced

1 tablespoon cumin seeds

SALSA:

14 ounces (400g) heirloom cherry tomatoes, diced

30 fresh mint leaves, chopped

2 tablespoons chopped fresh cilantro

Grated zest and juice of ½ lemon

2 tablespoons olive oil

Salt and fresh ground black pepper

7 ounces (200g) labneh, full-fat Greek yogurt, or sour cream

3.5 ounces (100g) feta cheese

1. Preheat the oven to 350°F (180°C).

2. Cut the zucchini in half lengthwise and scoop out the seeds, creating "boats." Finely chop the "guts" of the zucchini and set aside. Place the zucchini boats in a medium-sized bowl.

3. Pour 2 tablespoons of the oil over the zucchini boats and toss well to coat. Season the boats with a pinch each of salt and pepper and arrange them cut side up on a rimmed baking sheet. Roast until they're tender and offer no resistance when pierced with the tip of a knife, 20 to 25 minutes.

4. While the zucchini boats are roasting, make the filling: Put the chopped zucchini, shallots, garlic, cumin seeds, the remaining 2 tablespoons of oil, and a pinch each of salt and pepper in a medium-sized saucepan and cook over medium heat until you have a thick puree, about 15 minutes. (You're looking for the consistency of hummus; add water if the mixture becomes too thick.) Remove the pan from the heat.

5. Make the salsa: In a large bowl, mix the tomatoes with the mint, cilantro, lemon zest and juice, and oil until well combined. Season with salt and pepper to taste.

Nutrition per serving:		
Carb	Fat	Protein
13.6g	25.4g	10.2g

6. To assemble, spread a spoonful of the labneh on the base of each serving plate. Place three of the zucchini boats on top and fill them with a thin layer of the filling. Repeat with the remaining boats and filling. Top with the salsa, crumble the feta over the boats, and serve.

NOTE: *You can finely chop some of the zucchini boats if you need more filling.*

FOIL-WRAPPED SALMON WITH CUMIN-SPICED CAULIFLOWER RICE

SERVES 1

Some of my favorite dishes are the ones where everything goes in one parcel, and there's very little washing up to do afterward. Cooking meat or seafood in foil keeps all the flavors together and helps the protein stay tender and juicy.

¼ teaspoon cumin seeds

1 ounce (30g) watercress, roughly chopped, divided

1 cup (100g) riced cauliflower

Grated zest of ½ lemon

¼ teaspoon lemon juice

2 teaspoons olive oil, divided

Salt and fresh ground black pepper

1 (7-ounce/200g) skinless salmon or trout fillet, pin bones removed

1 ounce (30g) pitted green olives, sliced

1. Preheat the oven to 350°F (180°C).

2. Lightly toast the cumin seeds in a small skillet over medium heat until they just start to smell toasted, about 1 minute. Remove the pan from the heat and immediately transfer the seeds to a medium-sized bowl.

3. To the bowl, add half of the watercress, the riced cauliflower, lemon zest, lemon juice, 1 teaspoon of the oil, and a small pinch each of salt and pepper; mix well.

4. Place a 15-inch (40cm) square of wax paper on top of a 15-inch (40cm) square of heavy-duty aluminum foil. Spoon the cauliflower mixture into the middle of the wax paper. Season the fish with a pinch each of salt and pepper and set it on top. Fold the foil over the fish to enclose everything and fold the edges securely to seal the parcel.

5. Place the foil parcel in a 10-inch (25cm) square baking dish or on a rimmed baking sheet and bake until the fish can easily be pierced with a knife, 12 to 15 minutes. (Don't overcook, or the fish will dry out.) Remove from the oven and leave the fish to rest inside the sealed parcel for 3 minutes.

6. Dress the remaining half of the watercress with the remaining 1 teaspoon of oil. Season with salt and pepper to taste.

7. Gently transfer the contents of the parcel to a serving plate (or place the parcel directly on a plate, cut an X-shaped slit in the top of the parcel, and peel back the corners to reveal the contents). Arrange the dressed watercress on top of the fish, followed by the olives. Serve immediately.

Nutrition:		
Carb	Fat	Protein
5g	15.2g	38.5g

SOY-CURED SALMON WITH FENNEL AND CUCUMBER SALAD

SERVES 4

In this recipe, salty Asian-inspired salmon is complemented by a crisp, clean salad, and the warmth from the ginger and chili pepper are balanced by the coolness of the crème fraîche sauce. This is a make-ahead recipe, as the salmon needs to "cure" in the soy sauce for 24 hours. Since there's no heat applied, be sure to buy super fresh, high-quality salmon.

1 ounce (30g) grated ginger

1 clove garlic, grated

1 ounce (30g) green chili pepper, such as jalapeño, finely chopped

⅔ cup (150ml) soy sauce, tamari, or coconut aminos

1 (1-pound/500g) skinless salmon fillet, pin bones removed

4 ounces (120g) cucumber

3.5 ounces (100g) trimmed fennel bulb

1 tablespoon olive oil, plus more for drizzling if desired

Salt and fresh ground black pepper

½ cup (100g) Crème Fraîche Herb and Onion Sauce (page 216), for serving

1. Put the ginger, garlic, chili pepper, and soy sauce in a medium-sized bowl and mix well. Add the salmon, coating it thoroughly with the marinade. Cover tightly and refrigerate for 24 hours.

2. Remove the salmon from the fridge, rinse it under cold water, and pat it dry; discard the marinade. Cut the fish into slices about ¼ inch (6mm) thick and arrange on a serving plate.

3. Shave the cucumber and fennel using a mandoline or simply slice them very thinly with a sharp knife. Put them in a separate medium-sized bowl along with the oil and toss well. Season to taste with salt and pepper.

4. Arrange the salad next to the salmon. Serve with the crème fraîche sauce on the side, drizzled with a bit of olive oil, if desired.

Nutrition per serving:		
Carb	Fat	Protein
10g	14.8g	28.3g

NOTE: *Because the fish is not technically cooked, consume any leftovers within 3 days.*

ZOODLE CARBONARA

SERVES 2

Here's a riff on a traditional Italian carb-onara! (See what I did there?) This version is just as delicious but packs much less of a carb punch. This rich and savory dish makes a satisfying meal on its own; it is also a perfect side to a piece of grilled chicken or with a grilled chicken breast cubed and tossed right in. If you're a seafood lover, throw in some shrimp, which also pairs well with carbonara. *Note:* All of the ingredients in this recipe are Phase 1 friendly, but I've classified it as Phase 2 owing to the total carbs per serving.

---

7 ounces (200g) bacon, diced

2 cloves garlic, minced

½ cup (50g) finely diced shallots

1 cup (240ml) heavy cream

½ cup plus 2 tablespoons (50g) grated Parmesan cheese

Salt

14 ounces (400g) zucchini noodles (not frozen)

2 tablespoons olive oil, plus more if needed

Fresh ground black pepper

1 tablespoon chopped fresh parsley, for garnish

1. Cook the bacon in a medium-sized skillet over medium heat until crisp, about 5 minutes.

2. Add the garlic and shallots and cook until tender, another 5 to 10 minutes. (The bacon should have rendered enough fat, but add a little olive oil to the pan if the garlic and shallots stick to the bottom and start to burn. Keep an eye on it—garlic burns easily, and burnt garlic is very bitter.)

3. Pour in the cream and bring to a gentle simmer, then stir in the Parmesan and cook until it starts to thicken and coats the back of a spoon, 3 to 5 minutes. Remove the pan from the heat.

4. Bring a large saucepan of water to a boil over high heat. Add a generous pinch of salt and cook the zucchini noodles for about 90 seconds. (You want them to have a bit of bite to them, like al dente pasta. Cook them a little longer if you prefer a softer texture.)

5. Drain the zoodles well. (You can even dry them further by putting them on paper towels.) Transfer to a serving bowl and dress with the oil and a pinch each of salt and pepper.

6. Taste the sauce for seasoning and adjust as needed.

7. Top the noodles with the sauce, followed by a large pinch of pepper. Garnish with the parsley and serve immediately.

Nutrition per serving:		
Carb	Fat	Protein
12g	108g	20.9g

DAD'S SINGAPORE ZOODLES

SERVES 2

My father sometimes made this recipe when I was a kid. I had an adventurous palate even back then, and I still remember the fragrance of the spices as he was cooking and how impatient I was to taste the finished dish. He learned this dish from two culinary giants, Ken Hom and Delia Smith, and tinkered with their respective recipes over the years until he ended up with a version he could call his own. To this day I remain a huge fan of Singapore noodles—the blend of aromatics, the layers of flavor, the varied textures, the sweetness of the shrimp offset by the saltiness of the bacon, the finish of fresh cilantro, and the zing from the lime juice. There are several steps, but they're all pretty simple. Once you've tried your hand at it, I think you'll agree it's worth it.

1 ounce (30g) small dried shrimp (see Notes)

¼ cup (60ml) vegetable oil

3.5 ounces (100g) lardons or thick-cut bacon sliced crosswise into lardons

1 cup (100g) diced onions

1 tablespoon minced garlic

1 tablespoon grated or finely chopped fresh ginger

2 tablespoons curry powder (see Notes)

Salt

7 ounces (200g) poached chicken (see page 246) or any precooked, unseasoned chicken, shredded

2 ounces (50g) medium shrimp, peeled and deveined (see Notes)

7 ounces (200g) zucchini noodles (not frozen)

2 tablespoons soy sauce, tamari, or coconut aminos (see Notes)

FOR GARNISH/SERVING (OPTIONAL):

Thinly sliced scallions

Fresh cilantro leaves

Lime wedges

1. Soak the dried shrimp in a bowl of warm water for 30 minutes to rehydrate them (see photo on page 102). Drain the shrimp, reserving ½ cup (120ml) of the soaking water.

2. In a wok or large skillet, heat the oil over medium-high heat. When the oil is hot, add the rehydrated shrimp, bacon, onions, garlic, and ginger. Give it a good stir, then reduce the heat to low and cook gently until the onions become translucent and tender, about 15 minutes.

Nutrition per serving:		
Carb	Fat	Protein
14.8g	24g	79.5g

(recipe continues on page 103)

3. Add the curry powder and a pinch of salt and stir well.

4. Turn the heat down to medium and add the reserved shrimp water, chicken, and shrimp. Cook, stirring well, until the shrimp turn pink and white, about 5 minutes.

5. Add the zucchini noodles and soy sauce and mix well with a fork or a pair of wooden chopsticks (a spatula may cause the delicate zucchini noodles to break).

6. Serve immediately, garnished with scallions and/or cilantro and with a wedge of lime to squeeze over the noodles, if desired. This dish can also be served at room temperature.

NOTES: *One of the key ingredients that makes this dish sing is dried shrimp—little shrimp that have been dehydrated to concentrate their flavor. Be sure to use the tiny type with the paper skin on (xia pi in Mandarin). Rich in umami, these shrimp also lend a delightful crunch to the dish. For the other type of shrimp called for in this recipe, fresh raw shrimp works best, but you can also use frozen or precooked shrimp; just add them a couple of minutes later than suggested in step 4.*

Curry powder is the spice blend that gives this dish an intoxicating aroma, a great depth of flavor, and a beautiful golden turmeric hue. Ingredients vary from brand to brand, but as long as you get it from a reputable spice purveyor to ensure it's as fresh as can be, any formula will work. I prefer Madras-style curry powder, which is slightly spicier than most blends, but a milder blend is fine too.

For an extra dash of umami, replace 1 tablespoon of the soy sauce with fish sauce.

PAN-FRIED NY STRIP STEAK WITH CHARRED GREEN BEANS, ARUGULA, AND QUICK-PICKLED SCALLIONS

SERVES 1

Smoky green beans and tangy quick-pickled scallions prove that potatoes aren't the only good accompaniment to a juicy pan-fried steak. This hearty dinner rivals anything you'd get at an Italian trattoria. You can read more about how to create a perfect pan-seared steak out of a leaner cut like this on page 231 and, if desired, how to dry-age steak on page 227.

1 (7-ounce/200g) NY strip steak (about 1 inch/2.5cm thick)

0.7 ounce (20g) thinly sliced scallions

3 teaspoons red wine vinegar, divided

Salt and fresh ground black pepper

1 ounce (30g) green beans, ends removed

1.4 ounces (40g) arugula

1 teaspoon olive oil

3 tablespoons shaved Parmesan cheese

Maldon salt, for finishing (optional)

1. Remove the steak from the fridge and set it on the counter to come to room temperature.

2. Meanwhile, pickle the scallions: In a shallow bowl, combine the scallions with 2 teaspoons of the vinegar. Season with salt and pepper. Leave to marinate at room temperature for 20 minutes.

3. Heat a medium-sized heavy-bottomed skillet over medium-high heat. When hot, use tongs to hold the steak and press the fat cap on its side firmly onto the skillet. Once the fat is golden brown and a visible amount of fat has rendered, turn the heat up to high and brown both sides of the steak, about 2 minutes per side for medium-rare (130°F/55°C) (cook it slightly longer if you like it more well-done). Season with salt and pepper to taste and remove from the heat, leaving the skillet on the heat and keeping the fat in the skillet. Let the steak rest for 5 minutes.

4. Add the green beans to the hot skillet. Cook until they're nicely browned, 2 to 3 minutes. Add a few tablespoons of water and a small pinch each of salt and pepper and cook until the beans are tender and the water has evaporated, about 2 minutes longer.

5. To serve, put the arugula in a small bowl. Add the remaining 1 teaspoon of vinegar and the oil and toss well to coat. Season with salt and pepper to taste and place on a serving plate. Arrange the green beans on top. Slice the steak and layer it on the green beans. Top with the pickled scallions and shaved Parmesan. Finish with a pinch each of pepper and Maldon salt, if desired.

Nutrition:		
Carb	Fat	Protein
6g	31g	59.1g

BEEF TACOS IN LETTUCE CUPS WITH LIME CREMA

SERVES 1

I love a good taco, and this one doesn't disappoint! The lettuce cups cut through the richness of the beef, and you can make the filling as hot and spicy or as mild as you like. Serve with pork rinds and guacamole, if desired, or with corn tortilla chips for Phase 3. For those eating higher carbs, consider skipping the lettuce cups and serving the taco filling in a bowl over shredded lettuce or cauliflower rice, adding black beans. Cotija cheese is available at many supermarkets, but if you can't find it, you can use feta instead.

8 ounces (250g) ground beef

1 jalapeño pepper, membranes removed (see Note), chopped

½ clove garlic, crushed to a paste or minced

½ teaspoon ginger powder

1 cup (240ml) beef broth, homemade (page 266) or store-bought, or water

2 heads baby gem or 1 small head romaine or iceberg lettuce

Salt and fresh ground black pepper

3.5 ounces (100g) Cotija or feta cheese, crumbled, divided

LIME CREMA:

¼ cup (60g) sour cream

Grated zest and juice of ½ lime

Salt and fresh ground black pepper

1. Brown the ground beef in a large skillet over high heat, breaking it up into crumbles with a spatula, 6 to 8 minutes.

2. Stir in the jalapeño, garlic, and ginger powder. Cook for 1 to 2 minutes, until the spices have released their fragrances and are well incorporated, then pour in the broth and leave to reduce until the mixture is slightly thickened and glossy looking.

3. Meanwhile, separate the lettuce leaves. Reserve the smaller leaves at the core for use as taco shells. Halve the large outer leaves lengthwise, then slice them thinly crosswise. Add the sliced lettuce to the meat mixture and continue to cook for another 5 minutes.

4. While the meat mixture cooks, make the lime crema: In a bowl, combine the sour cream with the lime zest and juice, season with salt and pepper to taste, and set aside.

5. Season the beef mixture with salt and pepper to taste. Transfer it to a bowl and top with half of the cheese.

6. Build your tacos using an inner leaf as a shell, placing a spoonful of the meat in the middle. Dress with the lime crema and the rest of the cheese, wrap, and enjoy.

Nutrition:		
Carb	Fat	Protein
9.3g	81.7g	60.7g

NOTE: *Do not remove the membranes from the pepper if you like things spicy; the membranes are where the heat is.*

BLACK PEPPER CHICKEN RAMEN

SERVES 1

This light but punchy broth is packed with flavor and nutrients. Don't be shy with the black pepper; it really adds to the warmth of the dish.

7 ounces (200g) boneless, skinless chicken breast

2 cups (480ml) chicken broth, homemade (page 264) or store-bought

2 tablespoons soy sauce, tamari, or coconut aminos (regular or low-sodium)

1 tablespoon fresh ground black pepper, plus more for garnish

1 pod star anise

1 bay leaf

Salt

2 teaspoons unseasoned rice vinegar or red wine vinegar

3.5 ounces (100g) zucchini noodles (not frozen)

1 large egg, soft- or medium-boiled (see page 258) and halved

9 fresh cilantro leaves, chopped, for garnish

1. In a medium-sized saucepan, combine the chicken, broth, soy sauce, pepper, star anise, bay leaf, and a pinch of salt. Bring to a very gentle simmer, cover, and cook over medium heat for about 10 minutes, until the chicken is cooked through and the juices run clear when pierced. (The liquid should be barely bubbling; don't let it come to a rapid boil or the chicken will be overcooked and tough.) With tongs or a slotted spoon, transfer the chicken to a plate to cool.

2. Adjust the seasoning of the broth with salt and finish with the vinegar. Keep the saucepan on the heat, but cover it and reduce the heat to the lowest setting to keep the broth steaming hot but not simmering.

3. Once the chicken is cool enough to handle, shred it with two forks.

4. Place the zucchini noodles in a serving bowl and top with the shredded chicken. Strain the hot broth through a fine-mesh strainer right into the bowl, discarding the solids in the strainer. Arrange the egg halves on top and garnish with the cilantro and a pinch of pepper. Serve immediately.

Nutrition:		
Carb	Fat	Protein
8.5g	12.6g	60.2g

NOTE: *For additional flavor and visual interest, add a drizzle of toasted sesame oil or thin slices of scallion.*

SEARED TUNA WITH AVOCADO, CUCUMBER, AND TOMATO SALAD

SERVES 1

This refreshing dish speaks to the lighter side of keto. Watching your carb intake doesn't mean every meal has to revolve around fatty beef or pork. Lightly seared tuna that's soft and rare in the middle can really hit the spot. Using good-quality tuna will make this dish shine. Seek out fresh tuna because you're only searing the outside, leaving the inside rare. If you have a trustworthy fishmonger, consider buying a large piece that you can cut thick slices from and freeze the rest.

3.5 ounces (100g) peeled and pitted avocado

3.5 ounces (100g) cucumber

3.5 ounces (100g) heirloom grape or cherry tomatoes, halved

1 tablespoon plus 1 teaspoon Japanese-Inspired Dressing (page 210) or store-bought low-sugar or sugar-free sesame-ginger dressing

2 teaspoons olive oil

7 ounces (200g) fresh tuna, at room temperature

Salt and fresh ground black pepper

Maldon salt, for finishing (optional)

1. Make the salad: Slice the avocado and cucumber into sticks, about ½ inch (12mm) thick and 2 inches (5cm) long, and place in a small bowl. Add the tomatoes and dressing; toss well to coat and set aside.

2. Heat the oil in a small skillet over high heat. Season the tuna on both sides with a pinch each of salt and pepper. When the skillet is hot, sear the tuna, 60 to 90 seconds per side. Remove the pan from the heat and allow the tuna to rest for a few minutes before slicing. Cut the tuna on the bias, about ½ inch (12mm) thick, to reveal the rare center.

3. Arrange the salad on a serving plate and fan out the tuna slices on top for an artful presentation. If desired, finish with a pinch each of Maldon salt and pepper. Serve immediately.

Nutrition:		
Carb	Fat	Protein
6.3g	28.6g	32.9g

PHASE 1

GARLIC PRAWNS

SERVES 1

This is a great main dish for one, and it also makes a nice appetizer. To serve a crowd, simply double or triple the ingredient quantities. For a main meal, serve the prawns over Cauliflower Mash (page 172), steamed cauliflower rice, or zucchini noodles. For Phase 3, serve them over regular rice or pasta; linguine or fettuccine would work well here.

Leaving the heads and shells on helps the prawns cook evenly and keeps the delicate meat well insulated and less prone to becoming tough. Besides, eating shell-on prawns is a fun and delicious experience! I like to twist the head off and suck the sweet juice and tomalley out, then gently peel off the shell all the way to the tail to enjoy the succulent meat. This is a rewarding task that's a bit messy, so be sure to have a bowl of warm water to wash your fingers afterward.

---

2 tablespoons olive oil

1 clove garlic, minced or grated

Grated zest of ½ lime or lemon

Salt and fresh ground black pepper

7 ounces (200g) prawns or jumbo shrimp, heads and shells on

Juice of ½ lime or lemon

Roughly chopped fresh cilantro, for garnish

Maldon salt, for finishing (optional)

1. Place the oil, garlic, lime zest, and a pinch each of salt and pepper in a bowl large enough to hold the prawns; mix well.

2. Devein the prawns: Keeping the head, shell, and tail intact, use a paring knife to cut open the shell along the back of each prawn, slicing into the flesh just enough to expose the vein. Lift the vein out with the tip of the knife.

3. Add the prawns to the marinade and toss to coat. Leave to marinate at room temperature for 20 minutes.

4. Heat a grill pan or medium-sized skillet over high heat. When hot, put the marinated prawns in the pan and cook for about 90 seconds per side, until they turn pink and white. (The prawns must be cooked quickly over high heat or they will become chewy and dry. They will continue to cook after they're removed from the heat.)

5. Transfer the prawns to a serving plate and drizzle the lime juice over them. Garnish with cilantro leaves and finish with a small pinch of Maldon salt, if desired. Serve immediately.

Nutrition:		
Carb	Fat	Protein
4.5g	33.3g	41.5g

NOTE: *If you like, grill a few lime or lemon wedges along with the prawns and serve them with the prawns.*

CRISPY CHICKEN LEG QUARTERS WITH SESAME, SOY, AND LEAFY GREENS

SERVES 1

There's more to chicken than just boneless, skinless breasts! (1985 called; it wants its fat-free protein back!) Chicken thighs are highly underrated, particularly when you keep the skin on and let it get crispy. Plus, meat cooked on the bone is almost always more flavorful, tender, and juicy than a boneless piece, and it's difficult to overcook.

2 tablespoons olive oil

2 chicken leg quarters (about 1¼ pounds/600g)

Salt and fresh ground black pepper

2 tablespoons soy sauce, tamari, or coconut aminos (regular or low-sodium)

1 tablespoon unsalted butter

3.5 ounces (100g) stemmed and chopped kale

⅔ cup (30g) fresh spinach

1 tablespoon toasted sesame oil

1 teaspoon sesame seeds (see Note)

1. Preheat the oven to 350°F (180°C).

2. Heat the oil in a medium-sized oven-safe skillet over medium-high heat. Season the chicken with a pinch each of salt and pepper and place it in the pan, skin side down. Cook until the skin is golden brown and crispy, about 5 minutes, then turn it over and cook the other side for 3 minutes. Transfer the skillet to the oven and bake until the juices run clear when you poke the chicken between the leg and thigh with the tip of a knife, about 10 minutes.

3. Remove the skillet from the oven. Immediately coat the chicken on all sides with the soy sauce; transfer to a plate to rest.

4. Place the skillet over medium-high heat. Add the butter and kale to the pan and stir, scraping the bottom of the pan to release those lovely caramelized chicken bits—there's a ton of flavor there! Once the kale is wilted, about 3 minutes, add the spinach and cook for another 2 minutes, until the spinach is wilted. Season lightly with salt and pepper—go easy with the salt since the soy sauce is already providing some.

5. Add any of the chicken juices that have collected on the plate to the spinach and kale and finish with the sesame oil.

6. Arrange the greens on a serving plate, top with the crispy chicken, and finish with the sesame seeds. Serve immediately.

Nutrition:		
Carb	Fat	Protein
7.3g	52.6g	64.5g

NOTE: *If desired, you can toast the sesame seeds in a dry skillet over medium-high heat for a minute or two, until golden brown and nutty (watch carefully, as seeds burn quickly). Remove the seeds from the pan and set aside. You can do this while the oven is preheating and use the same skillet to cook the chicken.*

PAN-SEARED LAMB CHOPS WITH ROASTED VEGETABLES AND YOGURT MINT SAUCE

SERVES 1

This Middle Eastern–inspired dish highlights the classic pairing of lamb with yogurt and mint. The cool, creamy, and acidic yogurt is the perfect mate for seared fatty lamb; they go well with roasted eggplant and zucchini, which are traditional vegetables in this region. The Middle East is famous for grilled meats and vegetables—a low-carb dieter's paradise! (These vegetables and the yogurt sauce also pair well with the Roasted Rosemary and Garlic Leg of Lamb on page 140.) This is a meal on its own, but if you'd like to round things out further, pair it with cauliflower rice for low-carbers or regular rice or pita bread for those on Phase 3.

---

1 (3.5-ounce/100g) baby eggplant (aka Indian eggplant)

1 small zucchini (about 3.5 ounces/100g)

2 tablespoons olive oil

Salt and fresh ground black pepper

7 ounces (200g) lamb chops

Grated zest and juice of ½ lemon, divided

3½ tablespoons (50g) plain full-fat yogurt

3 tablespoons crumbled feta cheese

10 fresh mint leaves, chopped

1. Preheat the oven to 350°F (180°C).

2. Cut the eggplant in half lengthwise and score the flesh about ½ inch (12mm) deep. Cut the zucchini into sticks, about ½ inch (12mm) wide and 2 inches (5cm) long, and place in a bowl with the eggplant. Add the oil and toss to coat well. Season with a pinch each of salt and pepper.

3. Arrange the eggplant halves, cut side up, and the zucchini sticks in a single layer on a rimmed baking sheet and bake until golden brown, 20 to 30 minutes.

4. About 10 minutes before the vegetables are done, heat a small skillet over high heat. Season the lamb chops with a pinch each of salt and pepper. When the skillet is hot, use tongs to hold the chops and press them, fat side down, onto the bottom of the skillet to brown and allow some of the fat to render out. Then lay the chops on their sides and cook to medium-rare (130°F/55°C), about 3 minutes per side.

5. Transfer the lamb chops to a plate, drizzle with half of the lemon juice, and allow to rest for 5 minutes.

Nutrition:		
Carb	Fat	Protein
9.7g	79.5g	58.8g

6. While the lamb is resting and the vegetables are still baking, make the sauce: Combine the lemon zest, the remaining half of the lemon juice, the yogurt, feta, and mint in a bowl; season with salt and pepper to taste. (If you want a thinner sauce, stir in a bit more lemon juice.)

7. Serve the lamb chops and vegetables with the yogurt mint sauce on the side. Pour any juices from the lamb that have collected on the plate over the meat for extra flavor and enjoy.

KUNG PAO CHICKEN

SERVES 1

This is my take on the traditional kung pao chicken. I've omitted the nuts and taken out some of the higher-carb ingredients, but I guarantee you won't miss them—there's no loss of flavor here. For Phase 2, add 1 ounce (30g) of chopped peanuts or cashews for some extra crunch. Serve over cauliflower rice or zucchini noodles for Phase 1 or Phase 2; use regular rice or rice noodles for Phase 3.

2 tablespoons olive oil, divided

7 ounces (200g) boneless, skinless chicken breast, cut into cubes

Salt

½ teaspoon cracked Szechuan pepper or fresh ground black pepper, plus more if desired

¾ cup (75g) very thinly sliced celery

1 tablespoon sliced fresh red chili pepper, such as jalapeño or bird's-eye

1½ teaspoons thin matchsticks fresh ginger

½ clove garlic, thinly sliced

3 tablespoons chicken broth, homemade (page 264) or store-bought

2 tablespoons soy sauce, tamari, or coconut aminos (regular or low-sodium)

1 tablespoon plus 1 teaspoon unseasoned rice vinegar or red wine vinegar

1 heaping tablespoon thinly sliced scallions

9 fresh cilantro leaves

Maldon salt, for finishing (optional)

1. Coat the bottom of a wok or sauté pan with 1 tablespoon of the oil and place over medium heat.

2. When hot, add the chicken, a pinch of salt, and the Szechuan pepper and cook until the chicken develops a nice brown color, about 3 minutes.

3. Once the chicken is nearly cooked, add the remaining 1 tablespoon of oil, the celery, chili pepper, ginger, and garlic. Cook for another 2 to 3 minutes, tossing the pan occasionally.

4. Pour in the broth and soy sauce. Raise the heat to high and allow the liquid to reduce until it has thickened to a glazelike consistency, 2 to 5 minutes.

5. Stir in the vinegar, scallions, and cilantro leaves.

6. Taste for seasoning (if you're like me, you may want to stir in another generous pinch of Szechuan pepper or black pepper for an extra kick) and transfer to a serving plate. Finish with a pinch of Maldon salt, if desired. Serve immediately.

Nutrition:		
Carb	Fat	Protein
9.7g	7.3g	61g

PHASE
①

COTTAGE PIE

SERVES 2

This classic comfort food is traditionally topped with mashed potatoes. However, it's easy to substitute mashed cauliflower to get all of the flavor and none of the carbs. (Well, just a few carbs.) I've also provided a slightly higher-carb variation for Phase 2. Years of professional training have conditioned me to combine star anise, onion, and a bay leaf to give ground beef a depth of flavor that can't be beat. For Phase 3, consider adding a spoonful of miso paste and/or a meat paste, such as Better Than Bouillon or the famed British Bovril, to the meat mixture.

---

8 ounces (250g) ground beef

Salt and fresh ground black pepper

2 tablespoons olive oil

1 cup (100g) finely diced celery

½ cup (50g) finely diced onions

½ clove garlic, minced

4 sprigs fresh thyme

1 bay leaf

1 pod star anise

2 cups (480ml) beef broth, homemade (page 266) or store-bought

7 ounces (200g) Cauliflower Mash (page 172)

3 tablespoons (20g) grated Parmesan or shredded cheddar cheese (optional)

1. Brown the ground beef in a medium-sized sauté pan over high heat, breaking it up into crumbles with a spatula, 6 to 8 minutes. (Do this in small batches if you can so that the beef browns rather than boils in its own liquid. It does not need to be fully cooked at this point.) Season each batch with a small pinch each of salt and pepper.

2. Remove the browned beef from the pan and set aside. To the same pan, add the oil, celery, onions, garlic, thyme, bay leaf, star anise, and a pinch each of salt and pepper. Reduce the heat to low, cover the pan, and leave to sweat (cook without browning) for about 10 minutes, stirring occasionally to make sure the ingredients don't burn.

3. Once the celery and onions are tender, pour in the broth to deglaze the pan, using a wooden spoon to scrape the flavorful browned bits from the bottom of the pan.

4. Return the beef to the sauté pan, give the contents a stir, and cook, uncovered, for 60 to 90 minutes, until most of the broth has evaporated and the flavors have developed. Add a splash of water or a bit more broth if the mixture becomes too dry (there should be just enough moisture to cover the meat).

5. A few minutes before the meat mixture is ready, preheat the oven to 350°F (180°C).

Nutrition per serving:		
Carb	Fat	Protein
9.4g	44g	34g

(recipe continues on page 123)

6. Remove the thyme stems, bay leaf, and star anise pod from the meat mixture and discard them. Spread the beef mixture in an 8-inch (20cm) square baking dish or similar-sized oven-safe skillet and cover with the cauliflower mash. Sprinkle a pinch each of salt and pepper and the cheese, if using, on top.

7. Bake until golden brown around the edges, about 20 minutes. Let stand for 5 minutes before serving.

FOR PHASE 2:

Use 1 cup (100g) finely diced carrots in addition to or in place of the celery. Increase the diced onions to 1 cup (100g). Increase the cauliflower mash to 10 ounces (300g).

FOR PHASE 3:

Follow the directions for Phase 2, replacing the cauliflower mash with 10 ounces (300g) of mashed potatoes. To make the ultimate mash, use a good mashing potato (I like King Edward or Apache, but russet or Yukon Gold will work beautifully). Peel and quarter the potatoes and put them in a small saucepan filled with salted cold water. Bring to a boil and simmer for about 20 minutes, until you can pierce the potatoes easily with a knife. Drain well and return the potatoes to the pan. Add a heaping ¼ cup (60g) unsalted butter. (Yes, that much butter. While working for the legendary chef Joël Robuchon, I learned that he would add at least double that!) Mash until smooth and season to taste with salt and pepper.

ZUCCHINI LASAGNA

SERVES 2

A lasagna with no tomatoes and no pasta? Real Italians may want to burn me at the stake for this recipe, but I promise you it is as good as any lasagna you've ever had. If it bothers you to even consider this a lasagna, think of it as a savory meat casserole. With its hearty, aromatic beef and rich, creamy cheese sauce, this is pure indulgence minus the carbs. Use the Four-Cheese Sauce on page 198 or a store-bought cheese-based pasta sauce that's low in carbs.

8 ounces (250g) ground beef

Salt and fresh ground black pepper

2 tablespoons olive oil, divided

1 cup (100g) diced celery

½ cup (50g) diced onions

½ clove garlic, minced

4 sprigs fresh thyme

1 bay leaf

1 pod star anise

2 cups (480ml) beef broth, homemade (page 266) or store-bought

1 medium-large zucchini (about 7 ounces/200g)

⅓ cup (90ml) Four-Cheese Sauce (page 198) or store-bought low-carb cheese sauce

¼ cup (20g) grated Parmesan cheese

1. Brown the ground beef in a medium-sized skillet over high heat, breaking it up into crumbles with a spatula, 6 to 8 minutes. (Do this in small batches if you can so that the beef browns rather than boils in its own liquid. It does not need to be fully cooked at this point.) Season each batch with a small pinch each of salt and pepper.

2. Remove the browned beef from the pan and set aside. To the same skillet, add 1 tablespoon of the oil, the celery, onions, garlic, thyme, bay leaf, star anise, and a pinch each of salt and pepper. Reduce the heat to low, cover the pan, and leave to sweat (cook without browning) for about 10 minutes, stirring occasionally to make sure the ingredients don't burn.

3. Once the onions and celery are tender, add the broth to deglaze the pan, using a wooden spoon to scrape the flavorful browned bits from the bottom of the pan.

4. Return the beef to the pan, give the contents a stir, and cook, uncovered, for 60 to 90 minutes, until most of the broth has evaporated and the flavors have developed. Add a splash of water or a bit more broth if it becomes too dry (there should be just enough moisture to cover the meat).

5. A few minutes before the meat mixture is ready, preheat the oven to 350°F (180°C).

6. Slice the zucchini lengthwise into planks about ¼ inch (6mm) thick. Gently toss with the remaining 1 tablespoon of oil and season with a pinch each of salt and pepper. Char the zucchini on a grill pan or griddle over high heat. (Or use a skillet large enough to fit the zucchini planks in a single layer.)

Nutrition per serving:		
Carb	Fat	Protein
9.5g	44.6g	42g

7. Remove the thyme stems, bay leaf, and star anise pod from the meat mixture and discard them. Cover the bottom of an 8-inch (20cm) square baking dish or a 0.8-quart (0.8-liter) sauté pan with a layer of zucchini planks and top with one-third of the meat mixture. Alternate layers of zucchini and meat, aiming for three layers if possible and ending with zucchini. Top with the cheese sauce and Parmesan.

8. Bake until golden brown on top, about 25 minutes. Let stand for 5 minutes before serving.

FOR PHASE 2, increase the ingredient quantities as follows:

¼ cup (60ml) olive oil

1 cup (100g) diced carrots instead of or in addition to the celery

1 cup (100g) diced onions

10.5 ounces (300g) zucchini

¾ cup (180g) cheese sauce

MOUSSAKA

SERVES 4

This is a great dish to cook on a Sunday afternoon, pop in the fridge, and then reheat on a busy work night. Imagine treating yourself to hot, bubbly, cheesy comfort food at the end of a long day!

This recipe calls for ground lamb, but you can also use diced boneless leg of lamb or shoulder or ground beef.

4 tablespoons olive oil, divided

1 pound (500g) ground lamb

Salt and fresh ground black pepper

¾ cup (80g) diced onions

1 cup (100g) diced celery

3 cloves garlic, minced

2 tablespoons tomato paste

1 teaspoon dried oregano leaves

½ teaspoon ground cinnamon

1 bay leaf

1¼ cups (300ml) beef broth, homemade (page 266) or store-bought

2 tablespoons chopped fresh mint

2 medium eggplants (about 6 ounces/160g each)

1½ cups (360ml) Four-Cheese Sauce (page 198) or store-bought low-carb cheese sauce

Pinch of ground nutmeg

Beefsteak tomato slices, for garnish (optional)

1. Heat 1 tablespoon of the oil in a large, heavy-bottomed saucepan over high heat. When hot, cook the lamb, breaking it up into crumbles with a spatula and seasoning it with a pinch each of salt and pepper, until well browned, 5 to 6 minutes. Transfer the lamb, along with the pan juices, to a bowl and set aside.

2. To the same saucepan, add 1 tablespoon of the oil, the onions, celery, garlic, and a pinch each of salt and pepper; cook on low heat until tender and slightly browned, 10 to 15 minutes.

3. Add the tomato paste and cook for an additional 2 minutes.

4. Add the cooked lamb, oregano, cinnamon, bay leaf, and broth, cover with a lid, and cook until tender, 60 to 90 minutes. Add water or more stock if the mixture becomes overly dry (but go easy; you want it to hold together but not be swimming). Stir in the mint and remove from the heat. Remove and discard the bay leaf.

Nutrition per serving:		
Carb	Fat	Protein
9.7g	80g	22g

(recipe continues on page 129)

5. While the lamb is cooking, cut the eggplants lengthwise into planks about ¼ inch (6mm) thick. Drizzle with the remaining 2 tablespoons of oil, season with a pinch each of salt and pepper, and char on a grill pan or griddle over high heat, about 90 seconds per side. (Or use a skillet large enough to fit the eggplant slices in a single layer.)

6. Preheat the oven to 350°F (180°C).

7. Assemble the moussaka in a 10 by 7-inch (25 by 18cm) or similar-sized baking dish: start with a layer of eggplant, then a layer of the lamb mixture, alternating the layers and ending with eggplant. Cover with the cheese sauce and sprinkle the nutmeg across the top. If desired, lay a few tomato slices on top.

8. Bake until golden brown on top, 30 to 45 minutes. Let stand for 15 minutes before serving.

PERI-PERI CHICKEN

SERVES 4

This fiery chicken dish is originally from the African nation of Mozambique. It has been popularized by a chain restaurant, but you can replicate the flavors at home. It's worth using peri-peri (aka piri-piri) chilies, which can be found online and at some specialty stores. However, red jalapeños or another red chili variety, such as habanero, will do just fine. Consider serving this chicken atop cauliflower mash or with a crisp salad, which would be perfect for offsetting the heat.

Plan ahead here; the chicken needs to marinate for at least an hour. You may want to prepare a large batch a day or two in advance, so then all you'll need to do is cook the chicken.

---

7 fresh or dried peri-peri chilies or fresh red jalapeños

2 cloves garlic

Grated zest and juice of ½ lemon

½ cup (125ml) olive oil

1½ tablespoons red wine vinegar

1½ tablespoons smoked paprika

1 teaspoon dried oregano leaves

½ teaspoon salt

½ teaspoon fresh ground black pepper

4 chicken leg quarters (about 2½ pounds/1.1kg)

Lemon wedges, for serving

Maldon salt, for finishing (optional)

Fresh cilantro or parsley leaves, for garnish (optional)

1. Make the marinade: Chop the chilies and garlic into a fine paste (you can also use a food processor). Transfer to a large bowl. Add the lemon zest and juice, oil, vinegar, paprika, oregano, salt, and pepper to the bowl; mix well.

2. Separate the chicken drumsticks from the thighs by cutting through the joint connecting the two. Add the chicken to the marinade bowl and mix to coat well. Cover and refrigerate for at least 1 hour—preferably overnight—or up to 2 days.

3. Preheat the oven to 400°F (200°C).

4. Arrange the chicken, skin side up, in a large baking dish or a 12-inch (30cm) oven-safe skillet, reserving the marinade left in the bowl. Bake for 30 minutes, then brush with the reserved marinade. Raise the oven temperature to 425°F (220°C) and bake until the skin has a lovely dark char, the sauce is gently bubbling, and the juices run clear when you insert the tip of a knife into the thickest parts of the thighs and drumsticks, about 5 minutes longer.

5. Let the chicken rest for 5 minutes before serving. Serve with lemon wedges to squeeze over the chicken. If desired, finish with a pinch of Maldon salt and garnish with cilantro leaves.

Nutrition per serving:		
Carb	Fat	Protein
5.8g	38.9g	67.9g

NOTES: *For a milder dish, remove the veins and seeds from the chilies.*

To cook the chicken on a grill, preheat the grill to high, then lay the chicken, skin side down, on the grate and cook until the skin is crispy, about 15 minutes. Flip the chicken over and cook, basting with the marinade, until the internal temperature reaches 160°F (72°C).

POT-AU-FEU

SERVES 8

I can feel myself relaxing just thinking about pot-au-feu, a classic French dish of tender meat and vegetables cooked in a savory broth. Even for people not following a low-carb or keto diet, this dish is comfort food. Think of a Sunday night pot roast, your entire home filling with the aromas of cooking, and then sitting down to a meal that takes all your cares away. That's a tall order, but pot-au-feu delivers. You can make this recipe without brining the beef if you must, but the brine adds a lot of flavor and helps tenderize the meat.

1 (4½-pound/2kg) top round roast

1 batch All-Purpose Brine (page 268), cooled

10 peppercorns

1 sprig fresh thyme

1 bay leaf

8 medium carrots (about 1 pound/500g), peeled and halved lengthwise

4 large stalks celery (about 7 ounces/200g), halved crosswise

2 medium-large onions (about 6 ounces/170g each), peeled and cut in quarters from the root end

FOR SERVING/GARNISH (OPTIONAL):

Horseradish Cream Sauce (page 206)

Fresh ground black pepper

Fresh parsley leaves

1. Place the roast in a 5-quart (5-liter) container, preferably plastic. Cover it entirely with the brine. Let the meat brine in the refrigerator for 12 hours. When ready to cook, remove the meat from the brine and rinse; discard the brine.

2. Place the roast in a stockpot and cover with water—enough to cover the meat with some headroom for the vegetables. Add the peppercorns, thyme, and bay leaf. Bring to a gentle simmer over medium-high heat and skim off any fat or impurities that rise to the top.

3. Add the carrots, celery, and onions; reduce the heat to the lowest setting and cook, uncovered, for 3½ hours. Periodically skim off any fat that rises to the surface.

4. Remove and discard the bay leaf and thyme stem. Use a slotted spoon to transfer the vegetables to a bowl. Carve off a sliver of the meat while the roast is still in the broth and taste it. If the meat is not tender enough, cook for another 30 to 45 minutes. If the meat is ready, transfer to a carving board and carve against the grain into thin slices.

5. To serve, arrange the beef and vegetables on a high-rimmed serving plate. Ladle in some of the broth and, if desired, top with a dollop of horseradish cream sauce. Dust with a pinch of pepper and garnish with parsley leaves, if desired.

Nutrition per serving:		
Carb	Fat	Protein
8g	13.7g	51.2g

BACON AND BRIE BURGERS WITH ZESTY TOPPINGS

SERVES 4

Bunless burgers are a perennial go-to on a low-carb diet, and you can keep them as simple or make them as ultra-gourmet as you like. This one's a bit fancy, but you're worth it! Of course, you can always take things down a bit and use whatever cheese you have on hand, like cheddar, Swiss, or blue cheese. Use smoked cheese for a real treat or, for something off the beaten path, top each burger patty with a fried egg and some kimchi (page 192).

---

1 pound (500g) ground beef

Salt and fresh ground black pepper

1¾ tablespoons olive oil

8 strips bacon

3.5 ounces (100g) Brie

1.4 ounces (40g) pickled onions, homemade (page 190) or store-bought

1.4 ounces (40g) pickled jalapeño or pepperoncini, sliced

¼ cup (60ml) mayonnaise, homemade (page 208) or store-bought, for serving (optional)

1. Season the beef with a pinch each of salt and pepper and combine with your hands. Divide into 4 equal portions and form each into a patty, about 1½ inches (4cm) thick.

2. Heat a large skillet or griddle over high heat. Drizzle the burgers with the oil, then fry on both sides, 5 to 6 minutes per side for medium or 10 to 12 minutes for well-done.

3. Remove the burgers from the pan and set aside to rest. Using the same pan, cook the bacon over medium heat to your desired doneness.

4. While the bacon is cooking, slice the Brie and divide it among the cooked burgers, allowing it to melt on top.

5. Top each burger with 2 slices of bacon, pickled onions, and pickled jalapeño. Serve with mayonnaise on the side, if desired.

Nutrition per serving:		
Carb	Fat	Protein
2.1g	31.5g	32.2g

PHASE 1

SMOKED HADDOCK WITH HOLLANDAISE AND FENNEL BUTTER CABBAGE

SERVES 1

A marriage made in heaven! Poached eggs and smoked fish are no strangers to hollandaise sauce, and the nuttiness that the brown butter brings to this dish takes it to the next level. With buttery cabbage and aromatic fennel seeds, this is the epitome of a taste sensation. If you can't find smoked haddock, any other smoked white fish would work well here. Avoid using an oily fish like salmon, though, or the dish will be too rich. We certainly celebrate enjoying fatty foods on Phase 1, but there is such a thing as too much!

7 ounces (200g) smoked haddock

2 tablespoons olive oil

Salt and fresh ground black pepper

1 teaspoon fennel seeds

3½ tablespoons (50g) unsalted butter

1 cup (100g) finely shredded savoy cabbage

1 large egg, poached (see page 254) or soft-boiled (see page 258)

2 ounces (50g) Brown Butter Hollandaise (page 200)

1. Rub the fish with the oil and season with a pinch each of salt and pepper. Pour about 1 inch (2.5cm) of water into a saucepan large enough to accommodate a metal steamer basket and bring to a simmer over high heat. Steam the fish in the basket over the simmering water until it's tender (but not falling apart) and gives no resistance when pierced with the tip of a knife, 10 to 15 minutes. (If you don't have a steamer basket, place over the pan a wire rack that is large enough to rest comfortably on the rim of the pan but has squares tight enough to keep the fish from falling through. Put the fish on the rack and cover with a lid or foil to keep the steam in.) When the fish is done, remove it to a plate to rest.

2. While the fish is cooking, lightly toast the fennel seeds in a medium-sized skillet over medium heat until you begin to smell the anise aroma, about 1 minute. Add the butter, cabbage, and a pinch each of salt and pepper. Cook until the cabbage is wilted and tender, about 12 minutes.

3. While the fish is resting, warm up your poached or boiled egg in the steaming water for about 1 minute.

4. Spoon the cabbage onto a serving plate, place the fish on the cabbage and the egg on the fish (if using a boiled egg, slice it in half first), and spoon the hollandaise over the top. Serve immediately.

Nutrition:		
Carb	Fat	Protein
8.6g	84.9g	61.6g

SLOW-COOKED PORK RIBS

SERVES 2

These slow-cooked ribs aren't smoked like the ribs you'd find at a Southern BBQ joint, but they still bring big-time flavor. The meat needs to marinate for at least two hours, so you'll want to plan ahead. The steps, however, couldn't be easier: season, wrap, let sit in the fridge, and then bake! Red Cabbage Slaw (page 180) is a perfect accompaniment.

1 pound (500g) baby back pork ribs

1½ tablespoons English prepared mustard, like Coleman's, or Dijon mustard

1½ tablespoons Super Seasoning Blend (page 272)

1. Lay down two layers of heavy-duty aluminum foil large enough to cover the meat and place the ribs in the center.

2. Spread the mustard onto the meat, coating all sides. (It'll help the seasoning adhere, and the acid in it will help tenderize the meat.) Sprinkle the seasoning all over the ribs and wrap tightly in the foil.

3. Place in the fridge to marinate for at least 2 hours or up to overnight.

4. When ready to cook, preheat the oven to 285°F (140°C). Set the foil-wrapped ribs on a rimmed baking sheet and bake until the meat is tender and falling off the bone, about 2 hours 30 minutes.

NOTES: *When buying ribs, ask your butcher to remove the thin membrane that is attached to the underside, called the silverskin. The ribs will be more tender that way. To do it yourself, detach one corner of the membrane with the tip of a butter knife by about 1 inch (2.5cm). Grab the loosened membrane with a paper towel to get a better grip and peel it away from the rib rack in one piece.*

The ribs will be perfect straight from the oven. However, to add a pop of extra flavor, you can remove the foil once the ribs are done and finish them either under the broiler or on a grill for a few minutes until you get just a bit of char on the exterior.

Nutrition per serving:		
Carb	Fat	Protein
3.7g	46.3g	42.4g

ROASTED ROSEMARY AND GARLIC LEG OF LAMB

SERVES
4 to 6

Lamb is traditional for Christmas or Easter, but why wait for a holiday? This recipe is almost entirely hands-off cooking, so it's easy to make at any time of year. Leg of lamb is truly decadent, whether or not you're a low-carber. The lamb cooks low and slow, which renders the fat, leaving the meat incredibly tender and full of flavor. This dish pairs perfectly with Cauliflower Mash (page 172), Roasted Carrots (page 182), or cooked green beans. Of course, higher-carb eaters can have roasted or mashed potatoes on the side.

You can leave the anchovies out if you're not a fan, but I encourage you to give them a try; they lend an extra layer of flavor, and they melt into the meat rather than standing out on their own.

---

1 (3-pound/1.5kg) bone-in leg of lamb

2 cloves garlic, sliced

1 ounce (30g) salt-cured anchovies in oil, rinsed well and finely chopped

20 fresh rosemary leaves

Salt and fresh ground black pepper

2 cups (480ml) beef broth, homemade (page 266) or store-bought

1. Preheat the oven to 325°F (160°C).

2. Using the tip of a knife, make 8 to 10 slits in the lamb, about ½ inch (12mm) deep. Fill the slits with the sliced garlic, anchovies, and rosemary. Season the lamb with salt and a generous amount of pepper. (Remember that the anchovies will add more salt.)

3. Place the lamb on a rack in a roasting pan in which it fits snugly. Pour the broth over the lamb and cover tightly with foil.

4. Roast for 4 hours 30 minutes, basting the lamb with the broth every 45 minutes. Remove the foil for the last 20 minutes of cooking to get a nice golden color on the meat.

5. Allow the lamb to rest for 15 minutes before shredding it into large pieces and coating with the pan juices. Serve immediately.

Nutrition per serving, based on 6 servings:		
Carb	Fat	Protein
1.2g	20.5g	45.6g

ASPARAGUS WITH PROSCIUTTO, POACHED EGG, AND ARUGULA

SERVES 1

Asparagus and eggs scream "spring." It's the time of year I get most excited for. The produce available during this season includes some of my favorites, and asparagus, which is on the list of great nonstarchy vegetables, is right up there. (When asparagus is out of season, try replacing it with green beans or even peas and broad beans.) With salty prosciutto in the mix, this ensemble couldn't be better. (Well, if you want, finish it with a sprinkle of Parmesan cheese and it is even better!) This grown-up ham and egg dish is fantastic for a light lunch or dinner. To make it a more substantial meal, simply use more poached eggs.

2.8 ounces (80g) asparagus

Salt

½ cup (10g) arugula

3 tablespoons Simple Salad Dressing (page 212)

2 slices prosciutto

1 large egg, poached (see page 254)

Whole-grain mustard, for garnish (optional)

Maldon salt and fresh ground black pepper

1. If your asparagus is thick and woody, trim the ends and use a vegetable peeler to gently peel off the "eyes." If starting with the thinner, pencil-type asparagus, use as-is.

2. Fill a medium-sized saucepan with water and bring to a boil over high heat; stir in a generous pinch of salt and turn down the heat so the water is simmering gently. Add the asparagus and cook until you can easily pierce it with the tip of a sharp knife, 3 to 6 minutes, depending on the thickness of the spears. Remove from the water, pat dry with a paper towel, and arrange on a serving plate.

3. Put the arugula in a small bowl. Add the dressing and toss gently to coat. Place the salad next to the asparagus. Drape the prosciutto over the asparagus and carefully set the poached egg on top. If desired, drizzle whole-grain mustard on top. Finish with Maldon salt and pepper.

Nutrition:		
Carb	Fat	Protein
4.5g	52.8g	21.6g

CALAMARI WITH CHORIZO

SERVES
2 to 4

I have such fond memories of trips to San Sebastián in the Basque country in northern Spain, wandering down long, narrow alleys eating *pintxos*—a style of small bites similar to tapas. Plates of food are lined up on a bar; you help yourself, imbibe a splash of a local drink, and walk away smiling at the incredible quality and simplicity of the ingredients and the final dishes. Here is my variation on a bite I had in San Sebastián that can be served as a starter or a main course. This dish is proof that when you start with great raw materials, you don't need to do much to them; they shine on their own.

1 tablespoon plus 1 teaspoon olive oil

7 ounces (200g) Spanish chorizo, sliced ½ inch (12mm) thick or diced

1¼ pounds (600g) calamari or squid (bodies and tentacles), cleaned (see Note)

Salt and fresh ground black pepper

1 ounce (30g) fresh basil leaves, torn if large

Maldon salt, for garnish (optional)

1 lemon, cut into wedges

1. Heat the oil in a large skillet over medium heat. Add the chorizo and cook until the meat is slightly crisped and some of the fat has rendered, about 5 minutes.

2. Raise the heat to high and add the calamari. Season with a light pinch of salt and a generous amount of pepper. Fry for 3 to 5 minutes, keeping the squid moving in the skillet to ensure they cook evenly.

3. Transfer to a serving platter and garnish with the torn basil and a pinch of Maldon salt, if desired. Serve immediately, squeezing the lemon wedges over the dish before enjoying.

NOTE: *Freeze the seafood and then defrost it before cooking. This helps break down the protein and ensures a more tender finish. If you can't find small squid, use larger ones, sliced into finger-length strips and scored on the inside to make sure they cook quickly and stay tender.*

Nutrition per serving, based on 4 servings:		
Carb	Fat	Protein
8.6g	20g	37.6g

RUBY MURRAY CHICKEN CURRY

SERVES 4

Ruby Murray was a popular singer in Ireland and the U.K. in the 1950s. Somewhere along the way, the Cockney Brits started using her name as slang for a curry dish, to the point where, now, a Ruby Murray (or "a Ruby" for short) means curry. So consider this a good ol' Ruby Murray—one whose flavors and aromas will sing on your plate. This is a mild version, but feel free to go heavier on the fresh green chili if you prefer more heat. Cooking the chicken in the sauce creates a wonderful rich gravy that's ideal to serve over cauliflower rice (or regular rice for higher-carb eaters). Curry leaves can be found in the produce section of most South Asian grocery stores.

2 tablespoons vegetable oil, divided

8 bone-in, skin-on chicken thighs (about 2.2 pounds/ 1kg)

Salt and fresh ground black pepper

¾ cup (80g) thinly sliced onions

1 clove garlic, thinly sliced

2 teaspoons thinly sliced fresh ginger

0.5 ounce (15g) green chili pepper, such as jalapeño or serrano, sliced

2 tablespoons curry powder (preferably Madras-style)

1 teaspoon mustard seeds

1 (14.5-ounce/400g) can diced tomatoes, undrained

1 (13.5-ounce/400ml) can full-fat coconut milk

10 fresh curry leaves

2 tablespoons plain full-fat yogurt or sour cream, for garnish

1 tablespoon roughly chopped fresh cilantro, for garnish (optional)

1. Heat 1 tablespoon of the oil in a large, heavy-bottomed saucepan over high heat. Score the chicken skin. (This will help render some of the fat and add flavor to the sauce.) Season the chicken on both sides with a large pinch each of salt and pepper.

2. Brown the chicken in the pan, 2 to 3 minutes. (Just brown the surface; it will be fully cooked later.) Remove the chicken from the pan and turn the heat down to low.

3. Add the remaining 1 tablespoon of oil to the pan, then add the onions, garlic, ginger, and green chili. Cover the pan and leave to sweat (cook without browning) until the onions are translucent and tender, stirring occasionally to make sure the ingredients don't burn, 8 to 10 minutes.

4. Add the curry powder and mustard seeds and cook for 2 minutes, then stir in the tomatoes, coconut milk, and curry leaves.

5. Adjust the seasoning with salt and pepper, then return the chicken to the pan. Cover and cook over low heat until the meat is tender, 30 to 40 minutes.

6. Garnish with the yogurt, a pinch of pepper, and the cilantro, if using, and serve.

Nutrition per serving:		
Carb	Fat	Protein
9.6g	34g	30.4g

ZOODLE BOLOGNESE

SERVES 4

Spag bol! This is a perennial family favorite in the Parker household. There's something so nostalgic and comforting about slurping down pasta wrapped in a rich beef sauce—even when the "pasta" is zucchini! To make this a Phase 1 recipe, simply omit the carrots; for Phase 3, serve it over regular wheat pasta.

1 pound (500g) ground beef

Salt and fresh ground black pepper

2 tablespoons olive oil, divided

2 medium carrots (about 3.5 ounces/100g), diced

½ medium onion (about 3.5 ounces/100g), diced

½ clove garlic, minced

4 sprigs fresh thyme

1 bay leaf

1 pod star anise

2 tablespoons tomato paste

2 cups (480ml) beef broth, homemade (page 266) or store-bought

1 (14.5-ounce/400g) can diced tomatoes, undrained

1 teaspoon dried oregano leaves

1 to 2 strips Parmesan rind (optional)

14 ounces (400g) zucchini noodles (not frozen)

¼ cup (20g) shaved Parmesan cheese

1. Brown the ground beef in a large skillet over high heat, breaking up the meat into crumbles with a spatula, 6 to 8 minutes. Season with a pinch each of salt and pepper. (Cook the beef in small batches if you can so that it browns rather than boils in its own liquid. It does not need to be fully cooked at this point.) Remove the browned beef from the skillet and set aside.

2. To the same skillet, add 1 tablespoon of the oil, the carrots, onion, garlic, thyme, bay leaf, star anise, and a pinch each of salt and pepper. Reduce the heat to low, cover, and leave to sweat (cook without browning) until tender, stirring occasionally to make sure the ingredients don't burn, about 10 minutes.

3. Add the tomato paste and cook for another 2 minutes.

4. Pour in the broth and use a wooden spoon to scrape the flavorful browned bits from the bottom of the skillet. Then add the tomatoes, oregano, and Parmesan rinds, if using.

5. Return the beef to the skillet, cover, and cook, stirring occasionally, until the meat is tender and everything has come together cohesively, 60 to 90 minutes. Add a splash of water or stock if the mixture becomes too dry.

6. Once the meat is nearly finished, fill a medium-sized saucepan halfway with water. Bring to a boil over high heat and stir in a pinch of salt. Add the zucchini noodles and cook for 1 minute. Drain well, shaking off all of the excess moisture, and put in a medium-sized bowl. Add the remaining 1 tablespoon of oil and toss well to coat.

7. Divide the zoodles between four serving bowls. Remove the thyme stems, bay leaf, and star anise from the meat sauce and discard them. Spoon the sauce over the zucchini. Finish with the shaved Parmesan. Sprinkle with a pinch of pepper and serve.

Nutrition per serving:		
Carb	Fat	Protein
11.6g	45.6g	27.5g

FISH PIE

SERVES 1

It's hard not to love this recipe. It's so light and delicious, not to mention easy to put together. Another dish that proves low-carb diets include a world of food other than heavy steaks, burgers, and bacon—not that there's anything wrong with those foods! This recipe serves one, but you can easily scale it up for a family or a crowd.

1 (3.5-ounce/100g) skinless salmon fillet

1 (3.5-ounce/100g) skinless cod fillet

1 ounce (30g) trimmed fennel bulb, shaved or sliced very thinly

1 teaspoon chopped fresh parsley

3 tablespoons olive oil

Grated zest and juice of ½ lemon

Salt and fresh ground black pepper

7 ounces (200g) Cauliflower Mash (page 172), chilled

1. Preheat the oven to 350°F (180°C).

2. Cut the fish into bite-sized cubes and place in an 8-inch (20cm) square baking dish or 0.8-quart (0.8-liter) oven-safe sauté pan. Add the fennel, parsley, oil, lemon zest and juice, and a pinch each of salt and pepper and toss to coat the fish.

3. Spoon the cauliflower mash over the top of the fish mixture and spread it out so that it covers the fish. Bake until the top starts to turn golden brown, 20 to 25 minutes. Allow to rest for 5 minutes before serving.

Nutrition:		
Carb	Fat	Protein
15.6g	63g	43.5g

MEDITERRANEAN TROUT WITH CRUSHED PEAS AND TOMATO-RADISH SALSA

SERVES 1

The tomatoes and basil give this summery dish a wonderful Mediterranean feel. You can just imagine yourself sitting in the sun in the Tuscan countryside with a glass of crisp Pinot Grigio, reading a book while you enjoy this fish for a leisurely lunch.

Salt

¾ cup (100g) frozen peas

Grated zest and juice of ½ lemon, divided

1 tablespoon unsalted butter

Fresh ground black pepper

3.5 ounces (100g) heirloom cherry tomatoes, quartered

2 ounces (50g) radishes, quartered

3 tablespoons olive oil, divided

1 tablespoon red wine vinegar

9 fresh basil leaves, torn

1 (7-ounce/200g) skin-on trout fillet

Maldon salt, for finishing (optional)

1. Fill a medium-sized saucepan halfway with water and bring to a boil over high heat; stir in a pinch of salt. Add the peas and cook until tender, about 3 minutes. Drain off the water, keeping the peas in the pan. Add the lemon zest, butter, and a pinch each of salt and pepper. Using the back of a fork or a potato masher, crush the peas to a coarse mash. Keep warm.

2. In a bowl, toss the tomatoes and radishes with 1 tablespoon of the oil, the vinegar, and torn basil. Season to taste with salt and pepper; set aside.

3. Make several slashes on the skin side of the fish (this will help prevent it from curling up and allow the skin to get crispy). Season with a pinch of salt.

4. Heat the remaining 2 tablespoons of oil in a large nonstick skillet over high heat. Place the fish, skin side down, in the pan and cook until evenly browned and crispy, 3 to 5 minutes. Flip the fish over and cook until the flesh side is lightly browned and the meat is flaky at its thinnest part, 1 to 2 minutes. Remove the pan from the heat and squeeze the lemon juice into the pan. (It will finish cooking off the heat.)

5. Arrange the crushed peas in the center of a plate, scatter the salsa around that, and lay the fish, skin side up, on top. Serve immediately. Finish with Maldon salt, if desired.

Nutrition:		
Carb	Fat	Protein
22.5g	75.1g	47.8g

SEA BASS WITH LEMON BUTTER AND MASHED BROCCOLI

SERVES 1

This recipe is so simple—only four ingredients. It's light, full of flavor, and quick and easy to make. The crispy skin on the bass gives it a great texture, and the lemon butter melting over the top is mouthwatering. If you don't have a roll of lemon butter on hand, just use regular butter and a squeeze of fresh lemon juice. For extra convenience, use frozen broccoli florets and put them right in the boiling water; they'll cook even faster.

Salt

7 ounces (200g) broccoli, chopped into ½-inch (12mm) pieces

2 tablespoons olive oil, divided

Fresh ground black pepper

1 (7-ounce/200g) skin-on sea bass fillet

1½ tablespoons Lemon, Black Pepper, and Garlic Butter (page 222), sliced into rounds

1. Fill a medium-sized saucepan halfway with water and bring to a boil over high heat. Stir in a generous pinch of salt. Add the broccoli and cook until tender, 8 to 10 minutes.

2. Drain the broccoli and return it to the pan. Add 1 tablespoon of the oil and a pinch each of salt and pepper. Use the back of a fork to crush the broccoli into a coarse mash. Keep warm.

3. Prepare the sea bass: Make several slashes, about ½ inch (12mm) deep, on the skin side of the fish (this will help prevent the fish from curling up and allow the skin to get crispy). Season with a pinch of salt.

4. Heat the remaining 1 tablespoon of oil in a large nonstick skillet over high heat. Place the fish, skin side down, in the pan and cook until evenly browned and crispy, 3 to 5 minutes. Flip the fish over and cook until the flesh side is lightly browned and the meat is flaky at its thinnest part, 1 to 2 minutes. (It will finish cooking off the heat.)

5. Spoon the mashed broccoli onto the center of a plate, lay the fish on top, and arrange the sliced lemon butter over the fish. Serve immediately.

Nutrition:		
Carb	Fat	Protein
14.9g	42.8g	42.1g

FIVE-MINUTE SALMON

SERVES 1

I created this dish for a charity initiative started by the great chef Tom Aikens. I had five minutes to prepare something to raise money for an organization called Only a Pavement Away, which provides employment opportunities in the hospitality industry for people facing homelessness. I crept in and worked with what was available to me. So this recipe is quick to make, but more importantly, it's crazy tasty!

While this dish took me only five minutes of working at full speed (with all of the ingredients prepared for me in advance), with some planning, you can put together this simple meal very quickly, too.

2 ounces (50g) thinly sliced celery

2 ounces (50g) thinly sliced cucumber

2 ounces (50g) thinly sliced Granny Smith apple or jicama

2 ounces (50g) thinly sliced radishes

3.5 ounces (100g) heirloom grape tomatoes, sliced

3 tablespoons Japanese-Inspired Dressing (page 210) or store-bought low-sugar or sugar-free sesame-ginger dressing

1 teaspoon chopped fresh cilantro

1 teaspoon chopped fresh dill

1 teaspoon toasted sesame seeds

Salt and fresh ground black pepper

1 (7-ounce/200g) skin-on salmon fillet

1 tablespoon olive oil

1 tablespoon unsalted butter

1 lemon wedge

Maldon salt, for finishing (optional)

1. Prepare the salad: Combine the celery, cucumber, apple, radishes, and tomatoes in a large bowl.

2. In a small bowl, mix together the dressing, cilantro, dill, and sesame seeds. Pour over the vegetables; toss to coat. Adjust the seasoning with salt and pepper to taste. Place on a serving plate.

3. Prepare the salmon: Make 5 to 6 slashes, about ½ inch (12mm) deep, on the skin side of the salmon (this will help prevent the fish from curling up and allow the skin to get crispy) and dry it well with paper towels. Season with salt.

4. Heat the oil in a large nonstick skillet over high heat. Place the salmon, skin side down, in the pan and cook until the skin is golden brown and evenly crispy, 3 to 5 minutes. Flip the fish over, slip the butter underneath the fish before you lower it back onto the skillet, and cook until the flesh side is lightly browned but the center is still pink, 1 to 2 minutes, depending on the thickness. (It will finish cooking off the heat.)

5. Lay the fish on top of the salad. Squeeze the lemon wedge over the fish and, if desired, finish with a pinch of Maldon salt.

Nutrition:		
Carb	Fat	Protein
22.6g	97.5g	49.8g

TORTILLA PIZZA

SERVES 1

Low-carb pizzas have come a long way! Clearly this isn't your traditional Neapolitan-style pie, but traditions aren't all they're cracked up to be. With this ultra-quick recipe, not only do you not have to bother with making homemade dough, but the pizza is packed with flavor for a fraction of the carbs. (And it makes a super quick after-school snack for kids of all ages.) Get creative here: use whatever toppings you like, as long as you stay within your carb limit for the day. For a gourmet version, consider adding ricotta, grilled onions, and black olives. The world is your oyster...I mean, pizza!

---

1 (8-inch/20cm) low-carb flour tortilla or wrap

1 tablespoon tomato paste

1 ounce (30g) cooked bacon, cut into ½-inch (12mm) pieces

¼ cup (30g) shredded cheddar cheese

Salt and fresh ground black pepper

4 fresh basil leaves, whole or roughly torn

Extra-virgin olive oil, for drizzling (optional)

Maldon salt, for finishing (optional)

1. Set a rack in the middle of the oven. Preheat the oven to 350°F (180°C).

2. Place the tortilla on a rimmed baking sheet. Using a small rubber spatula or the back of a spoon, spread the tomato paste over the tortilla, nearly to the edge. Sprinkle on the bacon and cheddar. Season with a pinch each of salt and pepper.

3. Bake until the cheese is bubbling and the tortilla is crispy, 5 to 8 minutes.

4. Transfer to a serving plate, scatter the basil leaves on top, and finish with a drizzle of oil and a pinch of Maldon salt, if desired. Serve immediately.

Nutrition:		
Carb	Fat	Protein
14.3g	12g	26.1g

FISH CARPACCIO WITH RADISH AND SMASHED AVOCADO

SERVES 1

Fish carpaccio is one of life's wonders. The fish is lightly seasoned and finished with lime juice, which gently "cooks" it. Be sure to buy the freshest fish possible (see page 248), as this is still a raw dish. I use tuna loin, which I slice very thinly with a sharp carving knife. Alternatively, you can cut a slice around 1 inch (2.5cm) thick, lay it between two pieces of plastic wrap, and use a rolling pin to pound it thin.

3.5 ounces (100g) peeled and pitted ripe avocado

2 tablespoons crème fraîche or sour cream

Salt and fresh ground black pepper

1 (7-ounce/200g) skinless tuna, salmon, or mackerel fillet

3 ounces (85g) radishes, cut into thin wedges

Grated zest and juice of ½ lime

1 tablespoon extra-virgin olive oil

Maldon salt, for finishing

1. In a bowl, mash together the avocado and crème fraîche; season with salt and pepper to taste. Spoon the avocado mash onto the center of a serving plate.

2. Cut the tuna into very thin slices—about the thickness of a nickel.

3. Arrange the fish slices on top of the avocado mash in a single layer, overlapping slightly.

4. Scatter the radishes and lime zest on top of the fish; drizzle with the oil and lime juice. Finish with a pinch each of Maldon salt and pepper.

Nutrition:		
Carb	Fat	Protein
15.7g	61.1g	40.4g

PORK CHOPS WITH BRAISED CABBAGE AND MUSTARD-CHEESE SAUCE

SERVES 4

Pork and cabbage, great mates for life. Mustard-cheese sauce may sound a bit odd, but trust me; I wouldn't steer you wrong! Tender pork plus braised cabbage and the warming sauce is such an indulgent combination, and the peppery radish is the perfect thing to cut through the richness. This recipe is fine at any time of year, but just imagine tucking into it on a cold winter's night...

2 tablespoons unsalted butter, divided

4 (4-ounce/120g) bone-in, center-cut pork chops

Salt and fresh ground black pepper

1¼ pounds (600g) green cabbage, cut into 4 to 8 wedges (depending on the size of the head[s])

1 cup (240ml) chicken broth, homemade (page 264) or store-bought

1½ cups (360g) Four-Cheese Sauce (page 198) or store-bought low-carb cheese sauce

2 tablespoons whole-grain mustard

2 ounces (50g) radishes, thinly sliced

1 tablespoon olive oil

1. Preheat the oven to 350°F (180°C).

2. Heat 1 tablespoon of the butter in a large oven-safe skillet over medium-high heat. Season the pork chops on both sides with a pinch each of salt and pepper. Place them in the skillet and brown well on both sides, about 3 minutes per side. Remove the chops from the pan and set aside.

3. Melt the remaining 1 tablespoon of butter in the skillet. Add the cabbage wedges, season with salt and pepper, and repeat the browning process, about 3 minutes per side.

4. Once the cabbage is nicely colored, pour the broth into the skillet and pop it in the oven. Bake until the cabbage is tender and can easily be pierced with a knife, 15 to 20 minutes. Return the pork chops to the pan for the last 5 minutes of cooking.

5. While the cabbage and pork chops are cooking, put the cheese sauce in a small saucepan, stir in the mustard, and warm gently over medium heat.

6. Put the radish slices in a small bowl, add the oil, and toss well to coat. Season to taste with salt and pepper.

7. To serve, spoon some sauce onto each plate, place one-quarter of the cabbage and a pork chop on the sauce, and scatter the dressed radishes on top. Serve immediately.

Nutrition per serving:		
Carb	Fat	Protein
11.3g	58g	35.9g

SPICY MEATBALLS IN ROASTED TOMATO SAUCE

SERVES 4

Meatballs with a little kick to them—what could be better? Low-carb eaters can enjoy these over zucchini noodles, and those with a higher carb tolerance can have them over spaghetti. But don't dismiss the possibility of simply eating these on their own in a bowl with a sprinkle of Parmesan on top—nothing else needed! If you don't eat pork, you can use all beef here (or even swap in ground bison or turkey), but combining beef and pork is the classic Italian way.

8 ounces (250g) ground beef

1 pound (500g) ground pork

2 cloves garlic, grated

1 tablespoon smoked red chili flakes

1 tablespoon fennel seeds

Salt and fresh ground black pepper

6 teaspoons roughly chopped fresh parsley (leaves and stems), divided

2 tablespoons olive oil

2¾ cups (650ml) Roasted Tomato Sauce (page 218) or store-bought low-carb marinara sauce

1. Preheat the oven to 375°F (190°C).

2. Put the beef, pork, garlic, chili flakes, fennel seeds, a generous amount of salt and pepper, and 5 teaspoons of the parsley in a medium-sized bowl and combine well using your hands. Form the mixture into 1-ounce (30g) balls (this recipe should make about 24 meatballs).

3. Heat the oil in a large, heavy-bottomed saucepan or Dutch oven with an oven-safe lid over high heat. Working in batches, brown the meatballs on all sides (no need to cook them all the way through), then remove from the pan and set aside.

4. When the last batch of meatballs has been removed from the pan, pour in the tomato sauce and use a wooden spoon to scrape the browned bits from the bottom of the pan (there's a load of flavor there!). Turn the heat down to low, return the meatballs to the pan, and cover with a lid. Bake until the sauce has reduced and become a deeper red color and the meatballs have an even golden brown finish, 25 to 30 minutes.

5. Let rest for 5 minutes before serving. Garnish with the remaining 1 teaspoon of parsley.

Nutrition per serving:		
Carb	Fat	Protein
12.5g	60.5g	31.4g

MOULES MARINIÈRES

SERVES
4 to 6

Mussels are tasty little morsels to slurp down, and they're dynamite with crisp white wine if you are so inclined. They cook quickly and are so fresh-tasting, and this recipe creates the most amazing sauce that you can scoop up and drink like a soup. This dish can be served in a bowl on its own but also works well over zucchini noodles or linguine (watch the carbs, though, because the mussels alone have quite a bit of carbs). Higher-carb eaters may wish to use slices of crusty baguette to sop up the juices.

---

4 pounds (1.75kg) fresh mussels

1¾ tablespoons unsalted butter

1 cup (100g) thinly sliced celery

1 clove garlic, thinly sliced

Scant ½ cup (100ml) dry white wine

5.3 ounces (150g) crème fraîche

2 tablespoons chopped fresh parsley

Grated zest and juice of ½ lemon

Fresh ground black pepper

Lemon wedges, for serving

1. Wash the mussels under cold running water. Toss out any that don't close when tapped on a hard surface. Pull out any hairs and ensure the shells are clean of barnacles. Use a spoon to scrape off any impurities.

2. Heat the butter in an extra-large saucepan over medium heat. Add the celery and garlic, cover, and leave to sweat (cook without browning) until tender, stirring occasionally to make sure the ingredients don't burn, 8 to 10 minutes.

3. Turn the heat up to high, add the mussels and wine, cover, and steam until all of the mussels have opened, 3 to 4 minutes. Give the pan a shake every so often to redistribute the mussels and ensure they all open.

4. Keeping the burner on, pour the mussels into a large colander set over a bowl to collect the cooking liquid; discard any mussels that didn't open during cooking. Put the liquid back in the pan and bring to a boil, whisk in the crème fraîche, and reduce the heat to low. Add the parsley, lemon zest and juice, and a pinch of pepper. Stir in the mussels and serve immediately with lemon wedges.

Nutrition per serving, based on 4 servings:		
Carb	Fat	Protein
17.5g	24g	46.7g

NOTE: *The macronutrient breakdown for this recipe is based on a 50:50 meat-to-shell ratio.*

ROSEMARY BAKED CHICKEN WITH GREEN BEANS AND TOMATOES

SERVES 1

This is a simple one-pan dish with minimal prep and cleanup but maximum flavor. Simply toss all of the ingredients together and bake. You can easily scale up this recipe to make multiple servings. Consider using asparagus instead of green beans when it's in season.

---

7 ounces (200g) boneless, skin-on chicken breast

3.5 ounces (100g) green beans, ends trimmed

3.5 ounces (100g) heirloom grape or cherry tomatoes, halved

2 sprigs fresh rosemary

1 clove garlic, thinly sliced

1 tablespoon olive oil

Salt and fresh ground black pepper

2 tablespoons grated Parmesan cheese

1. Preheat the oven to 400°F (200°C).

2. Put the chicken, green beans, tomatoes, rosemary, and garlic in a medium-sized bowl. Toss with the oil and a pinch each of salt and pepper.

3. Spread out the green beans and tomatoes on a rimmed baking sheet or in a large oven-safe skillet. Place the chicken, skin side up, on top and bake until the skin is golden brown and the internal temperature taken in the thickest part of the breast registers 160°F (72°C), 25 to 30 minutes.

4. Finish with the grated Parmesan and serve immediately.

Nutrition:		
Carb	Fat	Protein
13.3g	25.4g	69.9g

SIDE DISHES

No pasta? No problem! Rice, potatoes, corn, and other higher-carb foods aren't included in Phases 1 and 2, but there's no limit to the fabulous side dishes you can make using nonstarchy vegetables. Plus, you can use some of these vegetables to re-create your favorite sides, minus the carbs. And creating your own dead-simple, low-carb sides is as easy as roasting, grilling, sautéing, or steaming your favorite vegetables and pairing them with one of the sauces or dips in this book.

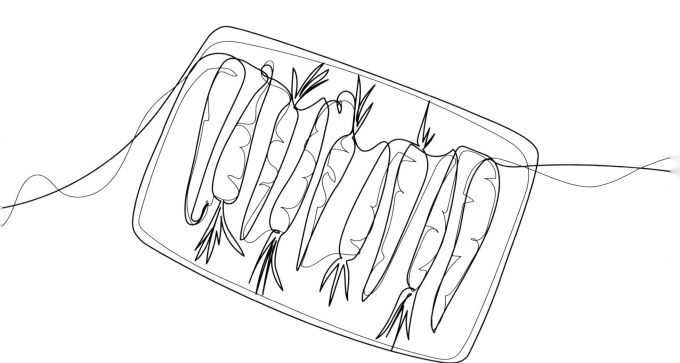

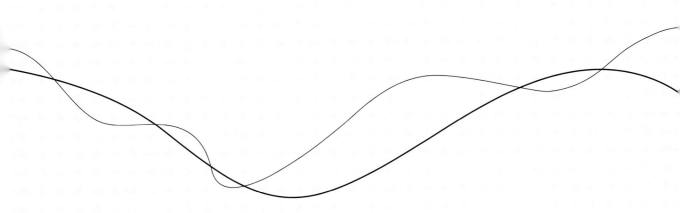

CAULIFLOWER MASH

SERVES 4

This is a simple recipe to master, and it's great to have up your sleeve because it comes together in minutes and can "plug and play" just about anywhere. Flag this page with a sticky note for quick access—but you'll have it memorized in no time, and you'll be able to make it without even looking. Just like mashed potatoes, cauli mash works well as a side to any roasted or grilled meat or fish. And once you're an old pro at this basic recipe, you can jazz it up any way you like—for example, add a splash of coconut milk and fresh cilantro for a Thai flair, or replace the butter with ghee and add some curry powder for an Indian twist.

6 cups (500g) small cauliflower florets

¼ cup (60ml) chicken broth, homemade (page 264) or store-bought

3½ tablespoons (50g) unsalted butter

FOR GARNISH (OPTIONAL):

Fresh ground black pepper

Sour cream or more butter

Crumbled cooked bacon

Snipped fresh chives or herb of choice

1. Place the cauliflower, broth, and butter in a microwave-safe bowl and cover with a lid or plastic wrap. Microwave on high until the cauliflower is fork-tender, about 6 minutes.

2. If you prefer a smooth texture, transfer the cooked cauliflower mixture to a blender and blend until smooth. (Be careful when blending hot foods.) For a chunkier texture, use a food processor and pulse the cauliflower to the desired consistency, or use a potato masher. (Add a generous spoonful of sour cream or heavy cream before blending or mashing to make this mash even richer. Blue cheese would also be dynamite if you're a fan.)

3. Serve as-is or garnish with a light pinch of pepper and a dollop of sour cream, some crumbled bacon, and/or some chopped chives or your preferred herb.

OVEN METHOD:

If you have a small microwave and want to cook a large batch all at once, it's better to cook the cauliflower in the oven. Start by melting the butter. Toss the cauliflower florets with the melted butter and roast in a 390°F (200°C) oven until the cauliflower is tender and gives easily when crushed with the back of a fork, 25 to 30 minutes. Remove from the oven and blend with the broth, salt, and pepper. The caramelization of the cauliflower will give this version a slightly darker color, but it will also provide a wonderful roasted taste.

Nutrition per serving:		
Carb	Fat	Protein
6.3g	10.1g	2.6g

BROCCOLI MASH

SERVES 4

Wondering what do with that lonely head of broccoli languishing in the produce drawer? Maybe it's even a bit past its prime? Kids won't eat their greens? This quick and easy recipe addresses all these issues. Broccoli mash adds a nice pop of color to a Sunday roast spread, and while it makes a great side dish, you can also reach for it as a snack. I love putting toasted nuts or seeds on top of just about anything, and they work especially well here, adding a nutty flavor and crunchy texture that make this a multi-dimensional dish. Get creative with it: add some plain fresh goat cheese before blending if you like a creamier mash, or, for an East Asian flavor, use toasted sesame oil and toasted sesame seeds instead of olive oil and pumpkin seeds. Feel free to use frozen broccoli florets in a pinch.

Salt

1 pound (500g) broccoli, roughly chopped

3½ tablespoons (50g) unsalted butter

0.7 ounce (20g) toasted pumpkin seeds (see Note, page 84), divided (optional)

Salt and fresh ground black pepper

2 tablespoons extra-virgin olive oil

2 tablespoons crumbled fresh goat cheese, for garnish (optional)

1. Fill a medium-sized saucepan with water and bring to a rolling boil over high heat. Add a generous pinch of salt and the broccoli and cook until very tender (soft enough to crush with the back of a spoon), 5 to 8 minutes.

2. Drain the broccoli and return it to the pan; allow the residual heat to evaporate the excess liquid.

3. For a smooth texture, transfer the cooked broccoli to a blender, add the butter and half of the pumpkin seeds, if using, and blend until smooth. (Be careful when blending hot foods.) If you prefer a chunkier texture, use a food processor and pulse the ingredients to the desired consistency, or use a potato masher.

4. Transfer to a serving bowl. Season with salt and pepper to taste. Garnish with the oil and, if using, the remaining pumpkin seeds and/or the goat cheese.

Nutrition per serving:		
Carb	Fat	Protein
11g	18.7g	4.2g

CAULIFLOWER RICE

SERVES 4

"Cauli-rice" is the secret to keto-fying any rice dish. Start with this basic recipe and change it up any way you like, from an East Asian fried rice to a Spanish paella or a Middle Eastern rice pilaf. This easily becomes a complete meal if you add some protein to it, but it's perfectly good under a saucy curry or as a simple side to a nice beef or pork roast. You can find both fresh and frozen riced cauliflower at most supermarkets now, but you'll pay a premium for it compared to making your own more economical version starting with a whole head of cauliflower. Consider making large batches and freezing some in flattened zip-top bags—that way you'll always have a stash on hand.

1 pound (500g) cauliflower, outer leaves removed

¼ cup (60ml) chicken broth, homemade (page 264) or store-bought

3½ tablespoons (50g) unsalted butter

Salt and fresh ground black pepper

1. Roughly chop the cauliflower and put it in a food processor. Run or pulse until it resembles the consistency of rice. (You can do this by hand with a knife if you're looking for a workout!)

2. Mix the riced cauliflower with the broth and butter in a large microwave-safe bowl and cover with a lid or plastic wrap. Microwave on high, stirring every 90 seconds, until the cauliflower just starts to become tender, 3 to 5 minutes.

3. Season with salt and pepper to taste and serve immediately.

Nutrition per serving:		
Carb	Fat	Protein
6.2g	10.1g	2.6g

CAULIFLOWER STEAKS

SERVES 1 to 2

Simple but delicious is the name of the game here. Cauliflower has such a mild flavor; it's the perfect vehicle to showcase the Smoky Chili and Garlic Salt. This unassuming vegetable doesn't always have to masquerade as rice or mashed potatoes on a keto diet—cauliflower deserves to shine on its own! This works well as a vegetarian main dish, too.

1 small head cauliflower

1½ tablespoons unsalted butter, melted

Pinch of Smoky Chili and Garlic Salt (page 271) or Italian or Cajun seasoning

1 tablespoon grated Parmesan cheese

1 tablespoon shelled sunflower seeds

2 tablespoons kale pesto, homemade (page 214) or store-bought, for serving (optional)

1. Preheat the oven to 350°F (180°C).

2. Remove the outer leaves from the head of cauliflower and cut 2 to 4 slices, about 2 inches (5cm) thick, from the center of the head, including the core. (Use the rest of the head for soup or cauliflower rice.)

3. Place the cauliflower steaks on a rimmed baking sheet and brush the melted butter over them. Season with the chili and garlic salt and bake until browned and tender, about 35 minutes.

4. Remove from the oven, sprinkle the steaks with the Parmesan cheese and sunflower seeds, then return the pan to the oven for an additional 5 minutes.

5. Serve as-is or pair with the kale pesto, if desired.

Nutrition, based on 1 serving:		
Carb	Fat	Protein
10g	23.9g	9.8g

RED CABBAGE SLAW

SERVES 2

Red cabbage often loses its color when cooked, but this dish keeps it raw and preserves its eye-popping vibrancy. Slicing the cabbage very thinly allows the lime juice and olive oil to soften it slightly but not so much that it loses its fresh crunch. This is a refreshing and palate-cleansing side that's perfect for pairing with rich dishes, like Slow-Cooked Pork Ribs (page 138) or roasted chicken (see page 242). There's a reason most BBQ joints have coleslaw on their menu!

2 cups (200g) thinly sliced red cabbage

Grated zest and juice of ½ lime

2 tablespoons extra-virgin olive oil

Salt and fresh ground black pepper

1 tablespoon finely chopped fresh cilantro

Lime wedges, for serving (optional)

Maldon salt, for finishing (optional)

1. Place the cabbage in a medium-sized mixing bowl. Add the lime zest and juice and the oil and season with salt and pepper to taste. Mix well to coat the cabbage evenly and let stand for 5 minutes.

2. Mix in the chopped cilantro. Serve immediately with a lime wedge or two and a pinch of Maldon salt as a finishing touch, if desired, or chill well before serving.

Nutrition per serving:		
Carb	Fat	Protein
8.2g	14g	1.4g

ROASTED CARROTS

SERVES 6

Step away from the lunchboxes! Carrot sticks make a simple after-school snack, but when you're all grown up, you might want something a little more interesting. This is a hassle-free way of cooking the best carrots you've ever had, perfect for serving alongside roasted chicken or even a good steak. This dish is delicious hot or cold, so consider making an extra-large batch for snacking on right out of the fridge.

1 pound (500g) medium-sized carrots (see Note), peeled

2 tablespoons olive oil

½ teaspoon salt

1 teaspoon fresh ground black pepper

4 sprigs fresh thyme

1 bay leaf

1. Preheat the oven to 350°F (180°C).

2. Cut a large square of heavy-duty aluminum foil (or two layers of regular foil) that is large enough to completely wrap the carrots. Place the foil on a rimmed baking sheet.

3. Place the carrots in the center of the foil, arranging them in alternating directions so they're tightly packed, like canned sardines.

4. Drizzle with the oil, sprinkle on the salt and pepper, and lay the thyme sprigs and bay leaf on top. Fold the foil tightly around the carrots and bake until they are tender and have no resistance when pierced through the foil with the tip of a knife, 30 to 40 minutes.

Nutrition per serving:		
Carb	Fat	Protein
8g	4.6g	0.5g

NOTE: *Medium-sized whole carrots that are sold in bunches with the tops intact are the best type to use here. The tops are delicious, too. If you want, you can roughly chop them and sprinkle them over the roasted carrots before serving.*

ROASTED BUTTERNUT MASH

SERVES 4

Butternut squash is popular in autumn, especially around Thanksgiving, but it's available year-round, and there's no reason not to take advantage of that. It can be prepared in so many ways. You can steam it or boil it, but roasting really brings out the sweetness and even a hint of nutty flavor. This super simple roasted butternut mash can be used as a side dish or eaten as a snack right out of a bowl. Pair it with turkey meatballs or a thick slice of meatloaf (sans breadcrumbs) and you've got a complete meal. It would also be excellent alongside a steak—baked potatoes aren't the only great steak accompaniment.

1 pound (500g) butternut squash, peeled and diced

1 tablespoon olive oil, plus more for drizzling if desired

Salt and fresh ground black pepper

3½ tablespoons (50g) unsalted butter

0.7 ounce (20g) toasted pumpkin seeds (see Note, page 84), for garnish (optional)

1. Preheat the oven to 375°F (190°C).

2. Toss the squash with the oil and season with a pinch each of salt and pepper.

3. Spread the squash on a rimmed baking sheet and roast until it is fork-tender and golden brown and caramelized on the outside, 40 to 50 minutes.

4. Place the squash in a food processor and puree, adding the butter after the squash starts to break down. (Use a potato masher if you don't have a food processor.)

5. Adjust the seasoning as needed. Transfer to a serving bowl. Top with the toasted pumpkin seeds and drizzle with olive oil, if desired.

Nutrition per serving:		
Carb	Fat	Protein
17.7g	15g	2.3g

ROASTED SWEET POTATO MASH

SERVES 4

This mash is a perfect partner for crispy pork belly (see page 238) or any other cut of pork, especially a thick-cut chop or a slice of pork loin or tenderloin medallions. It would also hold its own with roasted chicken or under a ladleful of hearty beef stew in winter. This recipe is strictly for Phase 3, but the lower-carb eaters in your household can have Roasted Butternut Mash (page 184) instead—you could easily make both at the same time since you'll have the oven on anyway! If you feel like something a little "moreish," as we say in South Africa, serve this topped with kale pesto. Kale and sweet potatoes are a match made in heaven.

1 pound (500g) sweet potatoes, peeled and cubed (see Note)

1 tablespoon olive oil

Salt and fresh ground black pepper

3½ tablespoons (50g) unsalted butter

3 tablespoons kale pesto, homemade (page 214) or store-bought, for serving (optional)

Maldon salt, for finishing (optional)

1. Preheat the oven to 375°F (190°C).

2. Spread the sweet potatoes on a rimmed baking sheet. Drizzle the sweet potatoes with the oil, season with a pinch each of salt and pepper, and toss to coat.

3. Roast the sweet potatoes until they are soft in the center and golden brown and caramelized on the outside, 40 to 50 minutes.

4. Place the cooked sweet potatoes in a food processor and puree, adding the butter after the potatoes start to break down. (Use a potato masher if you don't have a food processor.)

5. Adjust the seasoning as needed. Top with the kale pesto and finish with a pinch of Maldon salt, if desired.

NOTE: *Feel free to use any variety of sweet potato you like. Here, I've used Japanese sweet potatoes, the type with reddish purple skin, cream-colored flesh, and a chestnut-like flavor. They can be found at well-stocked Asian stores and some supermarkets. The regular orange-fleshed ones work well too.*

Nutrition per serving:		
Carb	Fat	Protein
26.1g	16.8g	3g

SMASHED CUCUMBER SALAD

SERVES 2

This tangy and refreshing dish employs the classic Chinese technique of smashing cucumbers before cutting them into bite-sized pieces for a salad, thereby creating an interesting craggy texture and allowing the vegetable to absorb more of the flavoring. This side salad is amazingly quick to prepare, and you can use it any way you like. If you like a little heat, add a pinch or two of red pepper flakes.

It's best to serve this dish immediately. You can make it in advance, but the moisture will start to leach out of the cucumber, which will make the dish more watery than is ideal.

1 large English cucumber (about 7 ounces/200g)

2 tablespoons toasted sesame seeds

1 tablespoon plus 1 teaspoon toasted sesame oil

1 tablespoon soy sauce, tamari, or coconut aminos

2 tablespoons unseasoned rice vinegar

Salt and fresh ground black pepper

1. Trim off both ends of the cucumber and quarter it crosswise. Lay the cucumber quarters on their sides. Take a large chef's knife and place the blade flat on top of each piece parallel to the cutting board and with the cutting edge away from you. Use the heel of your hand to press down on the blade just until the cucumber cracks open. Cut the smashed cucumber into bite-sized chunks.

2. Put the sesame seeds, oil, soy sauce, vinegar, and a pinch each of salt and pepper in a bowl (you can do this in the bowl you plan to serve in, if you wish—that'll be one fewer bowl to wash) and whisk until well combined. Add the cucumber chunks and toss to coat evenly. Taste for seasoning and add more salt and pepper if needed.

Nutrition per serving:		
Carb	Fat	Protein
4.2g	11.6g	2.2g

QUICK-PICKLED ONIONS

MAKES about
1 quart/640g
(1 tablespoon/
10g per serving)

Once you try these bright and tangy onions, you'll never want to be without a batch. They're perfect on a burger, with beef brisket, or with fatty pork—anything where a bit of vinegar can cut through the richness. You could even pair these with cream cheese spread over sliced smoked salmon—no bagel needed!

Feel free to use red, yellow, or white onions—whatever you like best.

¾ cup (200ml) red wine vinegar

⅔ cup (150ml) water

1 teaspoon coriander seeds

1 teaspoon mustard seeds

1 bay leaf

Salt and fresh ground black pepper

2 medium onions (about 5.3 ounces/150g each), thinly sliced

1. In a small saucepan, combine the vinegar, water, coriander seeds, mustard seeds, and bay leaf; bring to a boil over medium heat. Remove from the heat and add a generous pinch each of salt and pepper.

2. Place the sliced onions in a quart (liter)-sized jar and pour the pickling liquid over them. Allow to cool before you seal the jar and store it in the fridge for up to a month. (The onions will start to take on the pickled flavor after about 15 minutes, which is when they're ready, but they taste better to me after a week.)

Nutrition per serving:		
Carb	Fat	Protein
0.4g	0g	0g

KIMCHI

MAKES about
2 quarts/1.5kg
(scant ¼ cup/
50g per serving)

This recipe is the silver lining from an otherwise bad situation. I suffered a pulmonary embolism in 2020 and was hospitalized for an extended time, during which I was treated with strong antibiotics. When I was discharged, I was prescribed probiotics to help repopulate my friendly gut bacteria. I knew that fermented foods are loaded with probiotic bacteria, so I decided to try my hand at making them. Fermenting foods at home is so much fun—it's like being a magician in your own kitchen!

This kimchi recipe is one result from my fermentation journey, and it's as close to authentic Korean kimchi as it gets. It's pretty pungent, which is no problem if you live alone, but if you share a home—or a bed—with someone, be sure they like garlic and onions, too!

---

1 large head napa cabbage (about 4 pounds/1.75 kg)

¼ cup (65g) sea salt (see Notes)

4 ounces (120g) daikon, peeled

3 medium onions (about 5.3 ounces/150g each)

3.5 ounces (100g) scallions

10 cloves garlic, minced

1 teaspoon grated fresh ginger

2½ tablespoons (40ml) fish sauce (see Notes)

3 tablespoons Korean red pepper flakes (gochugaru)

1. Quarter the cabbage lengthwise. Remove the center core and slice the core finely; set aside. Cut the cabbage quarters crosswise into ½-inch (12mm) pieces (try to keep them as even as possible, as this will help ensure even fermentation).

2. Transfer the cabbage pieces (but not the sliced core) to a large mixing bowl. Sprinkle the salt over the cabbage and massage it well. (The salt will bring out some of the cabbage's natural juice. This process is critical for the fermentation.) Leave to sit for about 30 minutes.

3. Meanwhile, slice the daikon into matchsticks about ¼ inch (6mm) thick and 1 inch (2.5cm) long, then cut the onions and scallions into thin slices; set aside. In a large mixing bowl, mix the garlic, ginger, fish sauce, and red pepper flakes to form a paste.

4. Once the cabbage is ready, put a colander over a small bowl and drain the cabbage in the colander, letting the salty liquid fall into the bowl underneath. Use your hands to squeeze the cabbage dry. Set the liquid aside; you may need some of it for step 6.

Nutrition per serving:		
Carb	Fat	Protein
2.3g	0.2g	1.4g

(recipe continues on page 195)

5. Add the drained cabbage to the paste in the bowl along with the sliced cabbage core, daikon, onions, and scallions; mix thoroughly with your hands until the vegetables are thoroughly and evenly coated.

6. Transfer the mixture to a 2-quart (2-liter) mason jar or two 1-quart (1-liter) jars (or a fermentation crock if you have one). Press the mixture down firmly to express the liquid out of the vegetables and ensure that the contents of the jar are completely covered. If you need more liquid, use some of the reserved salty cabbage liquid.

7. Cover the jar(s) tightly and leave at room temperature for 5 to 12 days, depending on the ambient temperature of your kitchen (see Notes). Open the jar every couple of days to let the air out (this is called "burping") and then reseal. (You may wish to do this in the kitchen sink in case the contents expand—remember, this is a live ferment.) Taste the kimchi after 5 days. If it is to your liking, store it in the fridge. If you prefer it a little tangier, taste it the next time you "burp" the jar(s) and store it in the fridge whenever the kimchi is tangy enough for you (this shouldn't take longer than 12 days). It will keep for up to 3 months.

NOTES:

Sea salt is best here for flavor and texture. You don't want to use table salt or refined salts in this recipe because they contain iodine, which hinders the fermenting process.

Look for a fish sauce with no sugar or preservatives; the only ingredients should be fish (usually anchovies) and salt. Red Boat is a brand that fits this description.

This is a live ferment, so the ambient temperature will affect how long it takes to be ready. The warmer your kitchen (or wherever you stash the kimchi), the more quickly it will ferment; the cooler it is, the longer it will take.

DIPS, DRESSINGS, SAUCES, AND SPREADS

Having some favorite dips, dressings, sauces, and spreads can take your keto cooking from ho-hum to out of this world. When you find flavors and textures you love, make large batches to have on hand all the time. And get creative with how you use these sauces. Some are great for dipping pork rinds or cheese crisps on game day; others are good for celery or carrot sticks, jicama sticks, radish slices, or strips of bell pepper. And don't forget you can use these to jazz up plain proteins in a pinch. A tasty sauce or dip can elevate plain chicken breast or pork chops to something that will bring everyone to the table. Grill a few steaks in one go and keep them in the fridge. Slice them into strips to eat cold and you've got a protein-packed snack to dip into Horseradish Cream Sauce, Blue Cheese Dip, or Sour Cream and Chive Dip for a pittance of carbs.

FOUR-CHEESE SAUCE OR DIP

MAKES about
2 cups/480ml
(¼ cup/60ml
per serving)

Why have only one cheese when you can have four? The more the merrier! This rich and creamy sauce is perfect for a keto diet, but I guarantee the high-carb eaters in your life will love it just as much. It can be served warm or cold and works as both a sauce and a dip. (Want your kids to eat their veggies? Not a problem when they're covered in this sauce. The vegetables, that is, not your kids!) This sauce is also great for topping lasagna (see page 124) or as a cold dip for crudités at your next dinner party. Consider adding a spoonful of white miso paste; it deepens the flavor and provides even more umami. For an extra kick, add diced jalapeños or a few dashes of hot sauce, or sprinkle in some cayenne pepper or your favorite chili seasoning.

1¾ cups (400ml) heavy cream

3.5 ounces (100g) cream cheese

1 cup (110g) shredded mozzarella cheese

1 cup (110g) shredded cheddar cheese

½ cup (40g) grated Parmesan cheese

Salt and fresh ground black pepper

1. In a small heavy-bottomed saucepan over medium-high heat, bring the heavy cream and cream cheese to just below the boiling point.

2. Vigorously whisk in the other cheeses until melted and smooth. Season with salt and pepper to taste.

3. For a thicker consistency, reduce the heat and cook for a little longer to reduce the sauce, or, for a thinner consistency, simply add a few tablespoons of warm water.

4. Serve immediately while warm, or let the sauce cool down a bit and then place it in the fridge to chill. (Cover with plastic wrap directly on the surface of the cheese dip so it doesn't form a skin as it chills.)

Nutrition per serving:		
Carb	Fat	Protein
2.2g	35.7g	9.1g

BROWN BUTTER HOLLANDAISE

MAKES about
1 cup/240ml
(¼ cup/60ml
per serving)

A sauce made from egg yolks and butter: what could be more perfect for keto? Plus, hollandaise is a true culinary classic—one of the foundational sauces every chef learns to make. It is traditionally paired with poached eggs or fish, but it is also great on steak, especially with a little bit of finely chopped fresh tarragon for a truly French experience. While the traditional version is made with clarified butter, we're taking things further here by browning the butter just to the point where it takes on a delicious nutty flavor and a slightly darker golden hue. Note that hollandaise sauce doesn't store well, so it's best to make it as close as possible to the time you want to serve it.

½ cup plus 1 tablespoon (125g) salted butter

2 large egg yolks

1 tablespoon white wine vinegar

Salt and fresh ground black pepper

1 teaspoon lemon juice

1. Put the butter in a small saucepan over medium heat. Whisk continuously until it turns a nutty brown color. (Watch it carefully; butter can go from perfectly browned to burnt in only a few seconds.) Remove the pan from the heat and set aside.

2. Prepare a bain-marie: Half-fill another small saucepan with water and bring to a gentle simmer over medium heat. Combine the egg yolks and vinegar in a medium-sized heatproof bowl that will rest securely over the saucepan without its bottom touching the water. Whisk until the mixture starts to thicken and becomes pale, 3 to 5 minutes. Be careful not to overcook it or you'll make scrambled eggs! Look to get it to the ribbon stage, where you can lift the whisk over the mixture and create a figure-eight on the surface and it stays somewhat visible (or you can stick a wooden spoon in the sauce and lift it out, and the sauce will fall slowly from the spoon, back into the pot, creating what looks like a ribbon pattern).

3. Remove the egg yolk mixture from the bain-marie and slowly whisk in the brown butter, adding it little by little. Add a tablespoon of warm water if the sauce starts to look like mayonnaise, which means it has become too thick. You want the sauce to be smooth and thick but pourable; when you spoon it over a poached egg, it should fall slowly, draping over the egg like a silky, soft blanket. (Whisking in a little bit of warm water will also help prevent the sauce from splitting, which is when it loses

Nutrition per serving:		
Carb	Fat	Protein
0.5g	27.8g	1.5g

the emulsion and becomes grainy with a layer of butter fat on top. This can happen if you add the butter too quickly.)

4. Adjust the seasoning to taste with salt and pepper, stir in the lemon juice, and serve immediately.

BLUE CHEESE DIP

MAKES about
1 cup/240ml
(¼ cup/60ml
per serving)

People tend to have strong feelings about blue cheese: they either love it or hate it. If you're a blue cheese lover, this dip is for you! It's perfect for Crispy Chicken Wings (page 56) and also goes great with Roasted Carrots (page 182). For a kicked-up version, mix in a few dashes of hot sauce and a sprinkle of cayenne pepper. This dip is dynamite spread in a thin layer on sliced roast beef, and I wouldn't blame you for reaching into the fridge and taking a spoonful of it all by itself! You can also thin it with a little water and use it as a salad dressing.

---

7 ounces (200g) crumbled blue cheese

¼ cup (60g) sour cream

1 tablespoon white wine vinegar

Salt and fresh ground black pepper

Maldon salt, for finishing (optional)

1. Mix the blue cheese, sour cream, and vinegar until mostly smooth and well combined. You can use a blender, but the back of a fork works just as well. Season to taste with salt and pepper.

2. Keep refrigerated until serving. Serve cold with a pinch of Maldon salt, if desired.

Nutrition per serving:		
Carb	Fat	Protein
1.5g	14.7g	11.8g

SOUR CREAM AND CHIVE DIP

MAKES about
1¼ cups/300ml
(¼ cup/60ml
per serving)

This dip is the king of versatility and couldn't be quicker or easier to make. It pairs perfectly with several of the recipes in this book—my favorites are the Slow-Cooked Pork Ribs on page 138 and the Roasted Carrots on page 182. You can also serve it with fish, as a dip for crudités or pork rinds, or even with boiled eggs (see page 258).

1 cup (225g) sour cream

¼ cup (60ml) mayonnaise, homemade (page 208) or store-bought

1 tablespoon finely chopped fresh chives, plus more for garnish

Salt and fresh ground black pepper

1. Mix the sour cream, mayonnaise, and chives together in a small bowl until well combined.

2. Season with salt and pepper to taste. Transfer to a serving bowl and garnish with extra chopped chives.

3. Store the sauce in an airtight jar and keep refrigerated for up to 3 days.

Nutrition per serving:		
Carb	Fat	Protein
1.8g	17.3g	1.1g

HORSERADISH CREAM SAUCE

MAKES about 1 cup/240ml (¼ cup/60ml per serving)

Horseradish is a cousin to blue cheese in the "love it or hate it" realm. For those who enjoy the tongue-tingling (and sinus-clearing!) flavor, this horseradish cream sauce is perfect. When paired with hot or cold roast beef, it is a marriage made in heaven; this might even be the keto equivalent of peanut butter and jelly—a stroke of genius on the part of whoever first put them together. There's a reason why steakhouses always use this sauce to accompany prime rib or rib-eye steaks: the tanginess of the sauce is the perfect contrast to rich, fatty meats. But don't let that stop you from using this sauce on leaner meats and even on vegetables. To kick things up, consider adding some freshly grated horseradish root.

---

1 cup (225g) crème fraîche or sour cream

Grated zest and juice of ½ lemon

2 ounces (50g) cream-style horseradish or prepared horseradish

Salt and fresh ground black pepper

1. Mix together the crème fraîche, lemon zest and juice, and horseradish in a small bowl until well combined. Season with salt and pepper to taste. Garnish with extra pepper, if desired.

2. You can serve this sauce immediately, but if you're able to make it at least 12 hours ahead of time, the flavors will marry a bit more as the sauce sits in the fridge.

Nutrition per serving:		
Carb	Fat	Protein
3.4g	6.5g	1.2g

NOTE: *If you prefer a hotter version, add a bit more horseradish, or use less for a milder flavor. Read labels carefully when buying prepared horseradish. Avoid brands that contain sugar or corn syrup.*

HOMEMADE MAYONNAISE

MAKES about
3 cups/710ml
(¼ cup/60ml
per serving)

Fresh homemade mayo is a real treat. Once you've had it, you won't want to go back to store-bought. When you make it yourself, you can control the ingredients, especially the type of oil you use, and you can avoid the sugar, thickeners, and other additives the prepared stuff sometimes contains. A batch will last in the fridge for almost a week. This recipe yields a very thick mayo. For a thinner consistency, simply add a small splash of water when you prepare the mayo or follow the recipe as written and have people thin it out on their own before consuming it.

3 large egg yolks (preferably from free-range hens; see Note)

1 tablespoon Dijon mustard

Salt

1¾ cups (400ml) olive oil

2 tablespoons white wine vinegar

1 tablespoon lemon juice

1. Place the egg yolks, mustard, and a generous pinch of salt in a jar wide enough to insert an immersion blender, or the bowl of a small food processor. (If you have an immersion blender, I recommend doing this directly in the jar in which you intend to store the mayo—no bowl to clean! You can also use a mixing bowl and a whisk if you want a serious arm workout.) Blend/process or whisk together well.

2. With the immersion blender or food processor running, or while continuing to whisk, add the oil very slowly in a thin stream. Take your time. If you go too fast, the emulsion will break, and you'll be left with an oily, greasy mayo instead of the even consistency you're going for. (If this happens, try adding a tablespoon of warm water and keep blending.)

3. Finish by whisking or blending in the vinegar and lemon juice.

4. Taste for seasoning; adjust as needed. Store in a jar in the fridge for up to 5 days.

Nutrition per serving:		
Carb	Fat	Protein
0.2g	29.8g	0.7g

NOTE: *It's best to use egg yolks from free-range hens here because the yolks are consumed raw.*

JAPANESE-INSPIRED DRESSING

MAKES about 1½ cups/350ml (2 tablespoons/ 30ml per serving)

This salad dressing also goes well with hot or cold salmon, such as the Five-Minute Salmon recipe on page 156. For Phase 2 or 3, it's excellent as a dip for carrot sticks, or, for Phase 1, jicama and cucumber sticks or slices. For an especially nutty flavor, replace a small portion of the light sesame oil with toasted sesame oil. (You can easily find this at an Asian grocer, but many regular supermarkets carry it as well.)

½ cup (125ml) low-sodium soy sauce, tamari, or coconut aminos

¼ cup (60ml) untoasted (light) sesame oil

¼ cup (60ml) avocado oil or light olive oil

¼ cup (60ml) unseasoned rice vinegar

1½ tablespoons miso paste

1½ tablespoons wasabi paste

Salt and ground white pepper

1. Place the soy sauce, sesame oil, avocado oil, vinegar, miso paste, and wasabi paste in a jar with a tight-fitting lid and shake vigorously to combine. Season with salt and white pepper to taste.

2. Store in the refrigerator for up to 3 months. The dressing may separate over time. If this happens, simply give it a good shake to re-emulsify it.

Nutrition per serving:		
Carb	Fat	Protein
0.9g	7.5g	0.4g

SIMPLE SALAD DRESSING

MAKES about
1½ cups/350ml
(2 tablespoons/
30ml per serving)

Another quick make-in-the-jar keeper, this vinaigrette will add life to just about anything, so it's good to have a batch on hand in the fridge. Be prepared for it to become your new go-to all-purpose dressing. It has none of the sugar and preservatives often found in the store-bought stuff. When you start with good ingredients, you don't need anything extra!

1¼ cups (300ml) extra-virgin olive oil

2 tablespoons whole-grain mustard

1 tablespoon red wine vinegar

Generous pinch of salt and fresh ground black pepper

1. Place all the ingredients in a jar with a tight-fitting lid and shake vigorously to combine.

2. Store in the fridge for up to a week. Shake well before using.

Nutrition per serving:		
Carb	Fat	Protein
0.2g	13.7g	0.4g

KALE PESTO

MAKES about
2½ cups/600ml
(2 tablespoons/
30ml per serving)

This is a riff on the classic Italian pesto that typically calls for basil and pine nuts. Kale packs a bigger nutrient punch than basil does, and it goes great with pumpkin seeds, which not only are more economical than pine nuts but also lend a nutty flavor to the sauce. What can you use this pesto on? Whatever you like! Grilled chicken, vegetables...it's especially great paired with slices of goat cheese.

14 ounces (400g) stemmed and roughly chopped kale

2 ounces (50g) grated Parmesan cheese

2 ounces (50g) toasted pumpkin seeds (see Note, page 84)

1 clove garlic, peeled

Grated zest and juice of ½ lemon

1 cup (240ml) extra-virgin olive oil

Salt and fresh ground black pepper

1. Dry the kale fully by using a salad spinner or patting it with paper towels; water will dilute the pesto and change its consistency.

2. Place the kale in a blender or food processor along with the Parmesan, pumpkin seeds, garlic, lemon zest and juice, and oil; blend until the sauce is emulsified but still has a finely chopped texture. Season with salt and pepper to taste.

3. Store in an airtight container in the refrigerator for up to 3 days.

Nutrition per serving:		
Carb	Fat	Protein
2.4g	13.9g	2.3g

CRÈME FRAÎCHE DILL AND ONION SAUCE

MAKES about
¾ cup/150g
(2 tablespoons/
30g per serving)

This creamy sauce couldn't be easier to put together. It's perfect with rich fish and meats, such as salmon and pork belly, but you can pair it with anything you like. Boiled eggs (see page 258) come to mind, as do raw vegetables. If you're not a fan of dill, try this with cilantro instead.

½ cup (120g) crème fraîche or sour cream

1 ounce (30g) scallions, thinly sliced

2 tablespoons finely chopped fresh dill

Grated zest and juice of ½ lime

Salt and fresh ground black pepper

1. In a mixing bowl, combine the crème fraîche, scallions, and dill.

2. Add the lime zest and juice and mix to combine. Season with salt and pepper to taste.

3. Use immediately or store in an airtight container in the fridge for up to 3 days.

Nutrition per serving:		
Carb	Fat	Protein
3.1g	9.5g	1.7g

ROASTED TOMATO SAUCE

MAKES about 1 quart/1 liter (1 cup/240ml per serving)

You'll be amazed at the depth of flavor tomato sauce has when you take the time to roast the tomatoes first. This sauce is perfect for meatballs, meatloaf, or even braised lamb shanks—and, of course, for keto pizza or to top a bowl of zoodles! To give it some heat, add a pinch of red pepper flakes (or more than a pinch if you really want heat). Consider making a few extra batches in summer when tomatoes are at peak ripeness, as the sauce freezes beautifully. If you're making this sauce out of season, canned plum tomatoes will work just fine.

2.2 pounds (1kg) plum tomatoes, quartered lengthwise

1 cup (100g) finely diced shallots or white onions

4 cloves garlic, sliced

2 sprigs thyme

1 bay leaf

Scant ½ cup (100ml) olive oil

Salt and fresh ground black pepper

1. Preheat the oven to 375°F (190°C).

2. Place the tomatoes, shallots, garlic, thyme, and bay leaf in a 9 by 13-inch (22 by 33cm) baking dish. Drizzle with the oil and season with a pinch each of salt and pepper. Roast until the tomatoes are shriveled and blistered, 20 to 30 minutes.

3. Remove the dish from the oven and discard the thyme stems and bay leaf. Transfer the tomato mixture to a large, deep bowl and crush the tomatoes with a potato masher until you have a cohesive sauce.

4. Adjust the seasoning to your liking and serve immediately, or store in the fridge for up to 5 days for later use. To freeze the sauce, store it in heavy-duty zip-top bags in the freezer for up to 3 months. If you store them horizontally, you can stack up several bags in a small amount of space.

Nutrition per serving:		
Carb	Fat	Protein
10g	25.5g	2g

NOTE: *To speed things up, you can use a food processor, but if you prefer a chunkier, more rustic sauce, it's better to do it by hand, which will also retain its deep red appearance. Blending the sauce will give it a less appealing orange color.*

FLAVORED BUTTER TWO WAYS

Smoky Lime and Chili Butter

MAKES just
under 1 cup/
230g
(1 tablespoon/
14g per serving)

Lime is so underrated! It gets eclipsed by its more commonly used cousin, the lemon. But Mexican cuisine nails it with the heavy use of *chile limón*—chili with lime. It's a combination that can't be beat, and when you use it to flavor butter, well, now you've *really* got something. This flavored butter goes great with white fish, shrimp, and chicken. Pro tip: melt a generous pat of it to drizzle over a bowl of pork rinds. (You're welcome.) For Phases 2 and 3, you could even melt a pat of it to drizzle over a small bowl of roasted mixed nuts.

---

1 clove garlic, peeled

1 tablespoon smoked flaky salt

1 cup (227g) unsalted butter, softened

2 tablespoons cayenne pepper

2 tablespoons roughly chopped fresh cilantro

Grated zest and juice of ½ lime

1. In a mortar and pestle or a small food processor, grind the garlic and salt into a fine paste.

2. Put the garlic paste in a bowl along with the remaining ingredients; stir until well combined.

3. Place a square of plastic wrap or parchment paper on the counter. Use a rubber spatula to scrape every bit of the butter mixture into the center to form a rough log shape. Carefully roll into a smooth and even log and tie off the ends.

4. Store the butter in the refrigerator for up to 1 week or freeze for up to 3 months. Slice as needed for use.

NOTE: *This is the traditional way to prepare compound butter. Rolling it into a log shape makes for easy slicing and a nice presentation when you melt a lovely round of it on a steak or piece of fish. But you can also just store it in a covered bowl or sealed container in the fridge and use a fork or spoon to remove the amount you need.*

Nutrition per serving:		
Carb	Fat	Protein
0.8g	14.3g	0.3g

Lemon, Black Pepper, and Garlic Butter

MAKES just under 1 cup/ 230g (1 tablespoon/ 14g per serving)

The LBD, or little black dress, is the ace up a woman's wardrobe sleeve. It goes with everything; it's appropriate for a range of occasions from day to night; she feels comfortable in it; and it never fails. The same goes for LBG—lemon, black pepper, and garlic butter. These three simple flavors, when combined, will jazz up just about anything. This compound butter is especially delicious on grilled or pan-fried fish fillets or tossed with grilled broccoli, asparagus, or Brussels sprouts.

---

5 cloves garlic, peeled

1 tablespoon salt

1 cup (227g) unsalted butter, softened

2 tablespoons fresh ground black pepper

2 tablespoons roughly chopped fresh parsley

Grated zest and juice of ½ lemon

1. Using a mortar and pestle or a small food processor, grind the garlic and salt into a fine paste.

2. Put the paste in a bowl along with the remaining ingredients; stir until well combined.

3. Place a square of plastic wrap or parchment paper on the counter. Use a rubber spatula to scrape every bit of the butter mixture into the center to form a rough log shape. Carefully roll into a smooth and even log and tie off the ends.

4. Store the butter in the refrigerator for up to 1 week or freeze for up to 3 months. Slice as needed for use.

Nutrition per serving:		
Carb	Fat	Protein
1.1g	14.3g	0.3g

THE FOUNDATIONS

In this chapter, you will find a toolbox of great recipes and techniques that I have perfected over the years. These tried-and-true recipes have been designed to teach you how to bring the best out of basic ingredients. In fact, you're not simply learning to follow recipes here; you're developing transferable skills that, once mastered, will become springboards for new ideas and foundations on which to build countless dishes.

There are a few dishes and techniques that I think anyone who cares about cooking good food should have up their sleeve, whether you cook at home for yourself or your family or in a professional space for fine-dining patrons. A perfectly good low-carb meal can come together in minutes, or it can involve more extensive time investment and advance planning. There's no right or wrong, no good or bad; there's only what works for you and your lifestyle.

Most of the recipes in this book take only a little time to prepare yet still deliver maximum flavor and satisfaction. The recipes and techniques in this chapter are the exceptions. In following a low-carb diet and avoiding grab-and-go convenience foods that are loaded with sugar and starch, you're already going above and beyond what so many people do for their health and well-being. Why not learn these special techniques and go all out once in a while? *You're worth it!*

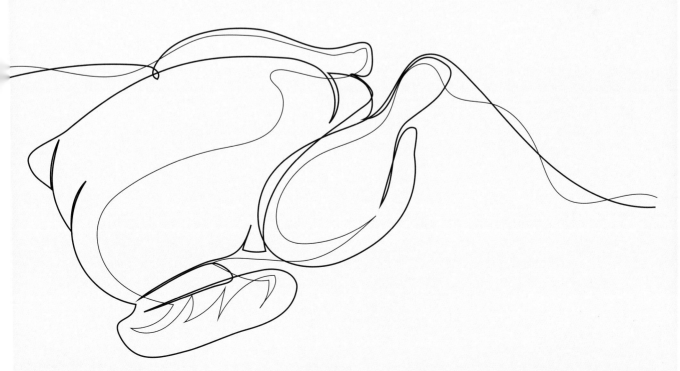

THE PERFECT STEAK

Whether you follow a low-carb diet or not, few foods are more satisfying than a perfectly cooked steak. Ask twenty chefs for their secret tips and you'll get twenty different answers, but one thing they'll all agree on is that a great steak starts with a great cut of meat. When you're trying to improve your health with a ketogenic or low-carb approach, the most important thing is to keep your carbohydrate intake low, and a fatty piece of beef certainly fits that requirement.

As someone who's been involved with food all my life, I encourage you to support small farms in your area. This is the best way to ensure that the meat you buy comes from animals that were raised humanely and in a way that helps to regenerate and rehabilitate the land rather than taking away from it. However, foods produced in this way can be cost-prohibitive for some people. If this is the case for you, simply buy the best quality that you can afford. My advice is to get to know your local butcher; Ryan Boon is mine, and he always has incredible meat, which is showcased in this book!

Cooking the perfect steak requires patience and just a little bit of know-how.

First, the steak must be dry. If you've bought a steak in a vacuum-sealed package, remove it from the package and pat it very dry with paper towels. If you have a little extra time, place it on a rack over a plate and refrigerate it, uncovered, at 35 to 41°F (2 to 5°C) until the surface is visibly dry on all sides, which should take two to four days. This will help dry the meat even further, which enables it to develop a nice crust. In old-school butcher shops and the world's finest steak-houses, beef is dried for an extended time because it allows even more excess moisture to leave the meat, which concentrates the flavors and even changes the meat a little bit biochemically.

This process is called dry aging, which is akin to maturing wine, where one needs to consider the humidity, temperature, and surroundings. Make sure that your refrigerator is within the target temperature range, don't disturb the humidity level by opening it too often or for too long, and keep other foods covered so the meat doesn't absorb their aromas. This process helps your steak become more tender and full-flavored in comparison to a steak that has not been dry-aged—to the degree that it is noticeable to you and your guests.

When the meat is nice and dry, you're ready to cook…*almost*. If time permits, take the steak out of the fridge at least twenty minutes before cooking. Starting with room-temperature steak will help ensure the formation of a gorgeous crust. If you try to sear a steak straight from the fridge when it's still cold, your pan will cool down too quickly. Moisture released from the steak will come to the surface and boil, and you'll end up with a "steak"—if you can call it that—that's an unappealing shade of gray and has been boiled in its own juices rather than seared on the surface. It's almost impossible to cook a steak to the proper internal temperature when the texture has been so radically altered.

Bottom line: if you're going for an appealing crust on a steak cooked to your preferred doneness—be it rare, medium-rare, or a little more well-done—start with a very dry piece of meat that you've allowed to come to room temperature. (Did I mention the crust also means *flavor*? Not only does the crust have a savory, caramelized flavor of its own, but it also helps the meat retain more of its juices and thus be more flavorful and tender. These extra steps are worth it if you have the time.)

There are numerous cuts of steak—some lean, some fatty, some with the bone in, and others that are boneless. There are no rules; cook what you like best. If you're new to cooking steak, though, as a general rule, meats that are cooked on the bone tend to be more flavorful than boneless cuts, and fat signals flavor. (And while you don't need to gorge on fat on a keto or low-carb diet, you certainly don't need to shy away from a nice fatty steak. Don't be afraid to go for a gorgeous marbled rib eye, a fatty T-bone or porterhouse, or a New York strip steak with a rim of fat on its side.) Thick steaks (1 inch/2.5cm thick or more) tend to stay juicier and more tender than thin ones. They are fabulous for showcasing a sear and perfect cooking technique, particularly when cooked rare or medium-rare.

HOW TO CHOOSE THE RIGHT STEAK FOR YOU

I often get asked which cut of steak I prefer and why. The truth is, each cut is perfect in its own right, and they all have a place in my kitchen and on my family's dinner table. That said, for me, first up is the tenderloin. As the name implies, it's the most tender cut you'll find; filet mignon, one of the best-loved steakhouse cuts, comes from the thinner end of the tenderloin that reaches into the short loin. It's typically one of the leanest cuts of beef. The tenderloin is great for steak tartare and even better for beef carpaccio. It's a great all-around piece of meat, but it's also the most expensive.

Next is the sirloin, aka strip steak or New York strip steak, which runs alongside the tenderloin. It has a fatty exterior but a leaner center. After that comes the T-bone steak. This cut from the short loin is the best of both worlds because it includes both the tenderloin and the sirloin, separated by the T-shaped bone—hence the name. The top cut of the T-bone is known as a porterhouse. It'll cost you a pretty penny, but it's worth it for a special occasion.

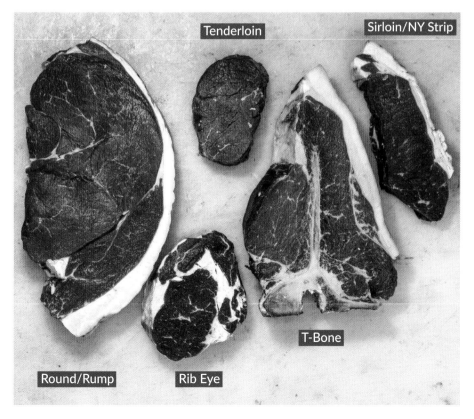

Then there's the rib eye, which, as the name suggests, comes from the rib portion. It's one of the fattiest cuts. Chefs and home cooks alike know that *fat means flavor*, and a rib-eye steak is no exception. Rib eyes are rich, hearty, and loaded with meaty, umami flavor.

Last is the round (aka rump), which comes from the muscles on the hind quarters of the steer. Because these leg muscles work so hard, round steaks are the toughest but also the leanest of all the primal cuts.

The following table shows the fat and protein content per 100 grams (3.5 ounces) of beef. It's a handy tool when designing recipes, and it might be useful for you when picking out steaks to cook at home or ordering in a restaurant so you can choose the cut that best suits your goals and nutritional needs.

Cut	Fat Grams Per 100g	Protein Grams Per 100g
Tenderloin/Filet	18	20
Sirloin	13	20
T-bone	15	19
Rib eye	22	24
Round	14.4	27.6

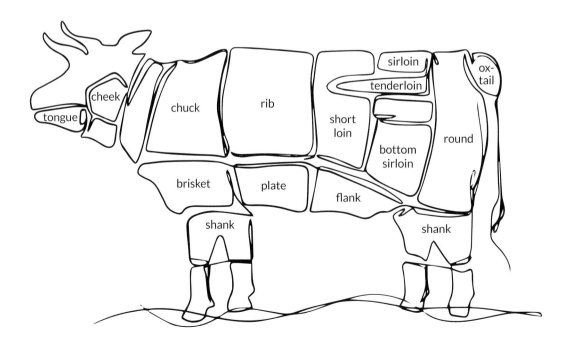

PHASE
①

PAN-SEARED STEAK

For lean cuts

When cooking a lean piece of meat, you need to use a bit of fat to lubricate the pan so the steak doesn't stick. First, preheat a heavy-bottomed skillet over high heat. (Cast iron works best, but a heavy stainless-steel pan is fine.) When the pan is hot, add a small amount of vegetable oil (choose a high-smoke-point oil, like canola or avocado oil; low-smoke-point oils, like extra-virgin olive oil, will burn too quickly and turn bitter), tallow, bacon fat, or ghee. While the oil or fat is heating up—let it get very hot—season the meat on both sides with salt and fresh ground black pepper.

When the fat starts to smoke, carefully place the steak in the pan, laying it down away from you, and *leave it*. You'll be tempted to shake or shimmy the pan or lift the steak to see how it's doing. *Don't!* You want the steak to stay in full contact with the pan so that it remains hot and cooks evenly. Leaving it where it is without poking or prodding it also allows a crust to develop. You'll want to give it a flip half-way through cooking to ensure that the meat cooks evenly and the crust is well developed on both sides. For a medium-rare steak, start with three to five minutes per side, depending on the thickness of your steak. Add intervals of ninety seconds per side if you prefer your meat closer to well-done. (See the following page for a visual guide to the levels of doneness. If you want a steak that will knock people's socks off—or, even if you're cooking for one, why not impress yourself?—a meat thermometer is your friend! See the temperature chart on page 233.)

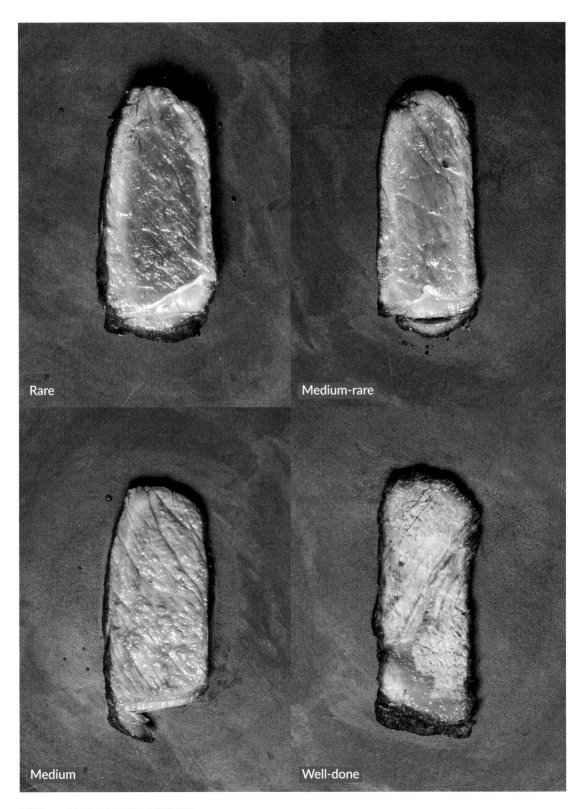

Rare

Medium-rare

Medium

Well-done

For fatty cuts

If you're cooking a fatty steak, you don't need to add extra fat to your cooking vessel. Simply heat a dry heavy-bottomed skillet over medium-high heat, season both sides of the meat with salt and pepper, and cook it as described above. If one side of the steak is a little fattier than the other, put the fattier side down first. When the fattiest side of a steak is the fat cap on its side, you'll want to hold the steak with tongs and press it down firmly onto the bottom of the hot pan to render the fat before lowering the steak onto the cut side. This allows you to not only use the meat's own fat to create the perfect cooking surface but also brown and crisp up the fat for extra flavor.

Resting

But wait! You're not done yet. There's one more step—a crucial one—to achieving a truly perfect steak. And that is the resting stage. Once the meat is cooked to your liking, remove it from the heat and allow it to rest on a cooling rack with a plate underneath to collect the juices. (You can discard this liquid if you like, but why not use it in a gravy or even a salad dressing?) The meat will continue to cook a bit on the inside, and letting it rest helps keep it tender. Depending on the size of the steak, I recommend leaving it for a minimum of five minutes.

Now, after the steak has rested, you are ready to make that first glorious cut and dig in!

The following table gives you the goal internal temperatures *after* the meat has rested. Since a steak continues to cook a little more after it's off the heat, remove it from the heat when it's two to five degrees Fahrenheit (one to six degrees Celsius) lower than the temperature suggested for your preferred level of doneness. An instant-read thermometer is essential here.

Doneness Level	Internal Temperature After Resting	
	Fahrenheit	**Celsius**
Rare	120°	45°
Medium-rare	130°	55°
Medium	140°	60°
Medium-well	150°	65°
Well-done	160°	70°

REVERSE-SEARED STEAK

Reverse searing is a foolproof method for cooking large cuts of meat. It's most commonly used on fatty beef or lamb. Don't try it with poultry or seafood— unless you want to end up with shoe leather for dinner, or possibly a terrible stomachache or a trip to the emergency room resulting from consuming undercooked chicken!

Reverse searing is simple. Instead of cooking a piece of meat at a very high temperature from the start, you cook it more slowly at a lower temperature and then give it a high-temperature sear at the end. This method has its pros and one con. The positives: it's a very consistent technique that will give you a wonderfully tender and eye-catching piece of meat; it's almost impossible to overcook the meat; and it helps render the fat, ensuring a crispy finish. The negative: reverse searing can take hours, so you have to plan ahead. It isn't a method you can decide to try at the last minute.

Let's say you've got a thick-cut, bone-in rib-eye steak, and you want it cooked medium-rare. Using the temperature chart on page 233, you would start by cooking it low and slow in a 130°F (55°C) oven. It could take anywhere from four to eight hours for the steak to reach an internal temperature of 130°F (55°C). (I assure you the steak will never be overcooked this way, as it will not get hotter than the temperature of the oven itself.) Once it hits your desired temperature, remove it from the oven, season it with salt and pepper, and sear it in a hot pan (or on an indoor or outdoor grill) over high heat to impart either a seared crust or grill marks.

The same reverse-searing technique can be used for larger quick-cooking cuts of meat, like top or bottom round roasts, sirloin tip roasts, and London broils. Because excessively high heat is not applied to the meat for a long time, the result is meat that is perfectly cooked all the way through and to the same degree from edge to edge.

GRILLED STEAK

Everyone needs to know how to grill up a tender and juicy steak. What would summer be without cookouts? Essentially, this method is very similar to cooking a steak in a skillet, so you will follow the same process when it comes to taking the meat out of the refrigerator at least twenty minutes early to come to room temperature and resting it after cooking. When using the barbecue, the skill lies in making the fire and controlling the heat.

If you are using a gas grill, the heat is easily controlled by simply turning the gas down or up.

For a charcoal grill, my advice is to make your fire on only one side of the vessel. This way, you can move the meat over if it is getting too hot or the fat is dripping down and causing flames to char the meat. You also need to ensure that your coals are white-hot. To test this, hold your hand over the grill. You should not be able to hold your hand 1 inch (2.5cm) away from the grill for longer than 1 second; you need that high heat to sear the meat. The same rule applies for a gas barbecue.

Then, unlike cooking a steak in a skillet, you will need to gently oil the meat for grilling, spreading a thin layer over the entire surface before seasoning the steak. I like to use canola or avocado oil here, but you can use any type of high-heat cooking fat you like. The cooking technique is the same as for pan-searing steaks, the only change being that you may get a kick-back of flames. I try to avoid this by simply moving the meat over to the side with no coals below the grate.

Once the meat is cooked to your desired doneness (see page 233 for temperatures), remove the steak from the grill and allow it to rest as directed previously.

THE PERFECT PORK BELLY

SERVES 6

Two words: PORK BELLY! Bacon isn't the only thing you can make from this fabulous, fatty, unctuous cut; you can braise it, confit it (slow-cook it in its own rendered fat), or poach it. In this case, we're roasting it, employing the brining technique, a foolproof way to get tender, juicy meat and crispy skin—the perfect contrast in textures—every time. (Plan ahead: the pork belly should be brined for two days.) Be sure to ask your butcher for a slab of pork belly with equal layers of meat and fat; a piece that is too fatty will not give you much of the succulent meat that this method produces.

I can't stress enough the importance of drying the rind after brining it in this recipe. Using a hair dryer may sound a step too far, but you won't regret it when you see the gorgeous and crispy crackling.

Serve the pork belly with roasted vegetables and a side of Cauliflower Mash (page 172) and Roasted Tomato Sauce (page 218).

---

1 (4½-pound/2kg) slab skin-on pork belly, about 4 inches (10cm) thick

2 quarts (2 liters) All-Purpose Brine (page 268)

1 medium onion (about 5.3 ounces/150g), cut into wedges

3 medium carrots (about 3.5 ounces/100g), peeled and halved lengthwise

1 tablespoon olive oil

Maldon salt

1. Place the pork belly in a 5-quart (5-liter) plastic container. Cover with the brine, making sure the entire slab is fully submerged. Refrigerate for 48 hours.

2. Preheat the oven to 325°F (160°C).

3. Remove the pork belly from the brine and discard the brine. Dry the pork skin thoroughly; you want it as dry as possible, as excess moisture will slow the process of the skin turning to crackling. (Pro tip: you can use a hair dryer to dry the skin!)

4. Using a sharp knife, make several slashes on the skin, about ½ inch (12mm) deep and ½ inch (12mm) apart. (These score lines will allow steam to escape during roasting and help ensure the skin gets crispy.)

5. Place the onion and carrots in a 9-inch (22cm) square baking pan. Lay the pork belly, skin side up, on top and rub the oil onto the skin, including all the nooks and crannies of the slashes. Season the skin generously with salt and roast for 1 hour 30 minutes to 2 hours, until the skin becomes puffy; if you tap a spoon on it, it will be rock solid and wonderfully crispy, and the meat below should be fork-tender. If the skin needs additional crisping, place it under a hot broiler for 3 to 5 minutes at a time. Watch it closely; it can go from perfectly crisp to burned quickly.

Nutrition per serving:		
Carb	Fat	Protein
6.3g	75.3g	78g

6. Let the pork belly rest for about 20 minutes before carving. To carve, I like to place the pork belly, skin side down, on a cutting board and cut it into slices about 2 inches (5cm) thick, gently pressing down on the knife to cut through the crispy rind.

THE PERFECT CHICKEN

As with the perfect steak, you can't cook a stellar chicken dish, especially roasted chicken, without a stellar bird. So how do you find one? Again, if you have the means to purchase a whole chicken directly from the local farmer who raised it, I encourage you to do so. But whether you get a chicken straight from a farmstand store, a farmers' market, or your regular supermarket, use at least three of your senses to tell whether it's a good candidate for this type of cooking: your sight, smell, and touch. (Taste would be nice, but unfortunately you can't use that until the bird is cooked!)

- **Sight:** Look for the chicken skin to have a nice pink color. If the chicken's diet included a lot of corn, it may have a yellow hue to it, which is fine. You want to avoid any bird that looks a little grayish. This signals an older bird, which may be better for stewing or using in a soup than for roasting. (Older birds will be very tough if roasted but soft and tender when stewed.)

- **Smell:** Fresh, raw chicken shouldn't have much of an odor. If a chicken smells foul or sour, it is likely past its prime.

- **Touch:** A whole, fresh chicken with the skin on should be dry to the touch. A slimy texture is bad news.

Of course, it's pretty difficult to touch and smell chickens at the market, and whole chickens are often sold in opaque packages. Fortunately, it's rare to come across one that's unsafe, so just make sure the packaging is intact and sealed properly. If you buy a frozen chicken, don't keep it in the fridge too long after defrosting; the same is true for a fresh bird. You'll notice changes in odor and texture if you let it sit in the fridge for a few days too many.

ROASTED CHICKEN

SERVES
4 to 6

It took me years to perfect this method, but after all that experimentation, I guarantee that this might be the best roasted chicken you've ever had. Full disclosure: it's not a quick recipe. (You'll want to start it two days before you plan to serve the chicken.) It takes some time, but in food, as in life, some things are worth the wait.

Beyond picking a good bird, the secret to a dynamite roasted chicken is brining, a technique that involves soaking meat in salted, seasoned water (sometimes mixed with vinegar) prior to cooking. Brining helps to flavor meats and ensures they stay tender and juicy. Follow the All-Purpose Brine recipe on page 268, and be sure to let the brine cool completely first because you don't want to cook the chicken in it!

Meanwhile, remove the wishbone: Feel for the Y-shaped bone just above the breasts, use a small paring knife to carefully score the entire length of either side of the bone, use your fingers to loosen it from the breast meat, grab the tip of the bone (where the two sides join together) with your fingers, and gently pry it out in one piece. (This step isn't required, but I recommend it because it will make carving the cooked chicken easier.)

Once the brine is completely cool, submerge the chicken in it, making sure the bird is completely covered. Leave the chicken in the brine in the fridge for eight to ten hours or overnight.

Even though you are brining the chicken to tenderize it and impart flavor, it will cook best and have the most appealing texture if it's very dry before cooking, just like a steak. (The golden-brown, crispy chicken skin that everyone goes nuts for is possible only if your chicken is dried before cooking.) So, after removing the bird from the brine, rinse it off and use paper towels to dry it all over as best you can. Next, place the chicken on a rack with a tray underneath and refrigerate it, uncovered, overnight. This will help dry the skin even further.

The next day, let the chicken come to room temperature—this will take about two hours, depending on the size of the bird. At this stage, you can truss the bird if you wish, which will allow it to cook more evenly and give it a better presentation once cooked. The images on the next two pages show the step-by-step process.

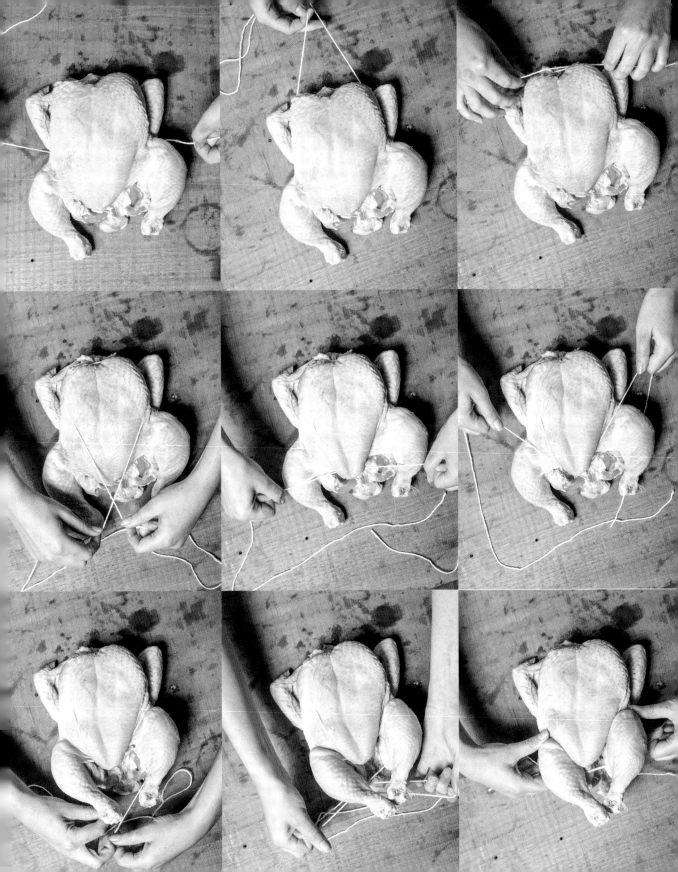

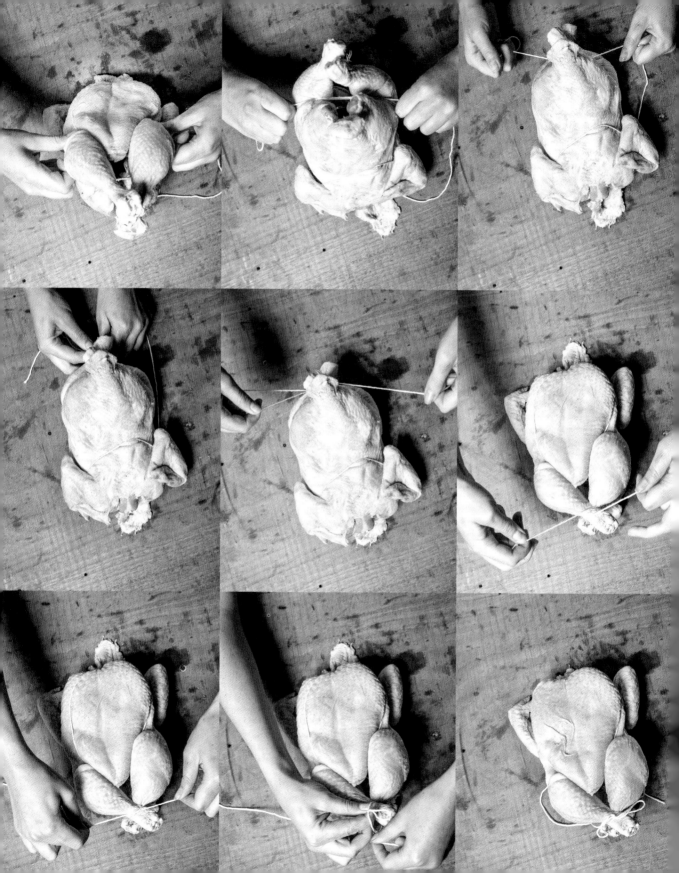

1 (5-pound/2.3kg) whole chicken, brined and dried

3½ tablespoons (50g) unsalted butter or ghee (clarified butter), melted

Salt and fresh ground black pepper

1. Preheat the oven to 425°F (220°C).

2. Brush the chicken with the butter and season all over with a pinch each of salt and pepper. Place on a rack in a roasting pan and roast for 20 minutes.

3. Lower the oven temperature to 400°F (200°C) and continue roasting the chicken until a meat thermometer registers 160°F (72°C) when inserted into the thickest part of the breast and the innermost part of the thigh, 30 to 45 minutes longer. Remove from the oven and allow to rest for 15 minutes before carving and serving.

POACHED CHICKEN

SERVES 4

I cook a batch of this chicken weekly. Precooked chicken is so convenient to have on hand for making any number of dishes: chicken salad, chicken chili, soups, stir-fries, fajitas, cobb salad, even pizza. And of course, chicken is the perfect zero-carb snack for grabbing straight from the fridge and eating on its own or with your favorite sauce or dip. This method is a two-for-one: you get the chicken and a flavorful broth to use elsewhere.

4 (5.3-ounce/150g) boneless, skinless chicken breasts

5 peppercorns

2 sprigs fresh thyme

1 pod star anise

1 bay leaf

1 tablespoon salt

1. Place all the ingredients in a large saucepan with just enough water to cover. Slowly bring to a gentle simmer over medium heat. Once simmering, turn down the heat to keep the water at a very low simmer, or approximately 175°F (80°C). Cook, uncovered, for 10 to 15 minutes. (It's important to go slowly so that the meat will be tender and juicy; if you let the poaching liquid boil hard, the chicken will dry out and become tough and chewy.)

2. If eating the chicken straightaway, use a slotted spoon to remove it from the poaching liquid and let it rest for 5 minutes before slicing and serving. (This will help the meat relax and ensure it is tender.) If you plan to serve it cold or to save it for another day, transfer it to an airtight container in the liquid and, once cool, store it in the fridge for up to 3 days. The poaching liquid can be used at least once more to poach another batch of chicken. You can also strain the "stock" and reserve it for other uses; it makes an excellent base for a soup or broth.

Nutrition per serving:		
Carb	Fat	Protein
0g	2.5g	54g

THE PERFECT FISH

A lot of people—even skilled home cooks—are intimidated at the thought of cooking fish. First, let's talk about how to identify a fresh fish, because fish must be fresh!

When it comes to whole fish, look for ones with bright, clear, and protruding (as opposed to sunken) eyes. The fins should be intact, and the skin should have a gentle glisten to it with no visible damage. Fresh fish shouldn't smell "fishy"; saltwater fish should smell like the ocean, and freshwater fish should smell like a clean pond. If a fish has cloudy eyes, damaged skin, dry skin with scales falling off, or a strong and off-putting odor, skip not just that fish but the whole fish counter and buy elsewhere.

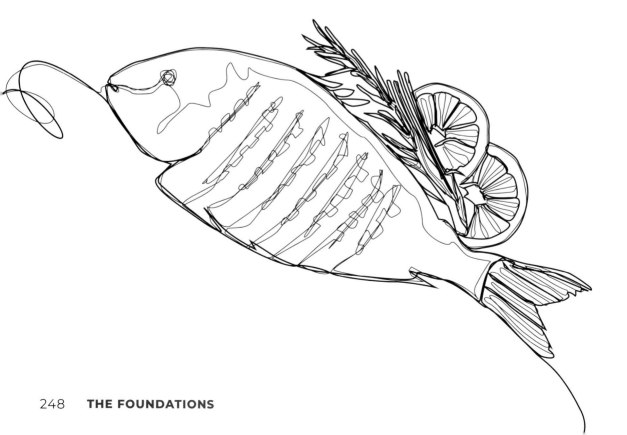

HOW TO FILLET A FISH

Fish fillets are easy to find, and they're convenient. However, when you have a beautiful whole fish that you've either caught yourself or bought from a good fishmonger, filleting it is a great way to get the portion sizes you want—and it's fun! Whether you are filleting a flat fish or a round fish, the following guidelines apply:

- Make sure your fish is well cleaned and wiped dry. A wet fish will slip all over your cutting board and make your task difficult and dangerous.

- Use a sharp filleting knife. This is a knife with a long, thin, and flexible blade, which bends easily and helps you get as close to the bone as possible.

- Stay close to the bone, using the natural bone structure of the fish to guide you. The closer you stay to the bone, the less meat you will leave behind.

- Always work from the head down to the tail and make sure you are cutting away from you. It's easy to cut through fish, and the last thing you want is a knife in the leg!

For flat fish

Unlike round fish, flat fish, such as flounder, halibut, turbot, and sole, don't have pin bones connecting two fillets to the main bone. Generally, they have four fillets—two on the darker top side and two on the bottom side. You want to fillet the top side first, as the natural outline on the darker side of the fish will help guide your first cut. Start by using scissors to trim off the gills and fins around the outside of the fish. Then, following the natural line on the fish skin (which is often clearly visible), make a cut from the head down toward the tail until you hit the middle point. Then turn your knife and, with the length of the blade against the bone, slice under the fillet all the way to the edge. This will free up the fillet, which can now be washed in ice water, dried, and set aside. Repeat the process with the remaining three fillets. Keep the bones for fish stock (see page 250).

For round fish

Generally, round fish have two fillets on either side of the bone structure with tiny pin bones that help attach the meat to the main bone. These include fish such as salmon, trout, hake, sea bass, mackerel, and many more. To fillet round fish, the same principles apply as flat; the difference here is that you work with the fish on its side and fillet horizontally. Start at the head and, working away from you, run your knife against the bone all the way down until you come through to the bottom of the fish, removing the fillet. Then, using a pair of fish tweezers, remove the pin bones. Wash and dry as directed above for flat fish.

HOW TO COOK FISH

When it comes to cooking fish, my advice is simple: regardless of the portion size you are cooking—a small fillet, a whole fish, or something in between—always remove it from the heat before you think it's fully cooked. Just like a steak, the internal temperature of the fish will rise a few more degrees as it sits. Use your meat thermometer to guide you here. You want to remove it at around 125°F (50°C). This way, it's unlikely to be overcooked when you serve it.

HOW TO MAKE FISH STOCK

Fish stock is a great way to use fish bones and reduce food waste. The process is a lot faster than that for chicken broth (page 264) or beef broth (page 266). All you need to do is slice 2 stalks of celery, 1 onion, 1 fennel bulb, and 1 leek, then sweat the vegetables in vegetable oil in a stockpot over low heat until tender. After about 15 minutes, add 2 cups (480ml) of white wine and reduce down, then add your chopped, washed fish bones, ½ bunch of fresh parsley, and 1 bay leaf and cover with water. Bring to a boil and skim the fat, turn down the heat, and simmer for 20 minutes. Remove the pot from the heat, then pass the stock through a fine-mesh strainer lined with a few layers of cheesecloth (this will ensure that any impurities are strained out). It will keep in the fridge for up to 3 days or will freeze well for up to 3 months.

THE PERFECT EGG

Eggs are a low-carb dieter's best friend! (Assuming you're not allergic, of course.) One large egg has a negligible amount of carbs while packing 7 grams of complete, high-quality protein. Eggs also provide several key vitamins, minerals, and other helpful compounds. The yolks contain highly bioavailable lutein, which is good for eye health, and are the richest source of choline in most people's diets. (Choline is a critical nutrient for the brain and nervous system. Your body makes choline on its own, but why not goose things along a bit and give it some extra?)

Eggs are among the most versatile ingredients you can keep in your kitchen. They work in sweet or savory dishes. They can be consumed as a meal all by themselves, be the star of a dish (like a quiche or frittata), or play a supporting role (like in a cobb salad). And they can be eaten in solid form (an omelette or scrambled eggs) or liquid form (hollandaise sauce). Not many other foods can boast that résumé!

Fresh eggs work best in most recipes. How do you know if your eggs are fresh? If you're able to source eggs from a nearby farm, you can trust that they're likely only a few days old. If you buy them from a store, the three-digit Julian date on the carton tells you the pack date (usually the same day the eggs were laid), and that gives you some idea of how old the eggs are. To know for sure whether an egg is fresh, the test is quick and easy: Carefully place the egg in a bowl of water. If it sinks to the bottom and lies on its side, it's very fresh. If it floats at an angle or stands on end, it's a little older, but still fine to eat. If it floats to the top, it's old and should be discarded.

For most egg dishes, whatever eggs you have on hand will be fine. You may just wish to have these tidbits in the back of your mind because fresh eggs are the best for poaching but tend to be very hard to peel when boiled. The reason is that eggshells are a tiny bit porous, which means that air can pass through them. Fresh eggs have little to no air in them, so they're heavier; that's why they sink. Eggs that have been sitting around a while contain more air, so they tend to float. This is also why eggs that are not as fresh are easier to peel after boiling: the small amount of space allows you to get under the shell better.

Eggs are simple ingredients, yet they can be prepared in a dizzying array of styles. Because they're so simple, it's natural to downplay their importance and assume they're easy to prepare. Eggs are, in fact, a common proving ground for new or young chefs. One of my first jobs in London was cooking breakfast in a five-star hotel. The head chef there was *not kidding around*. Before service each day, I had to prepare an array of egg dishes to present to him and wait for his nod of approval before I was deemed competent enough to cook for the guests.

That might have been a bit much, but there was a method behind the madness. Cooking eggs is an exercise in balance: a few seconds too long and the yolk is too firm; a few seconds too short and it could end up raw. The good news is, *you* don't have to walk through that gauntlet. I'm going to share with you my never-fail methods for cooking the perfect egg six different ways so you'll have plenty of options for these perfect low-carb gems.

POACHED EGGS

Use fresh eggs when poaching. If you use older ones, the yolks will not stay in the middle, and they will overcook before the whites have cooked. (Not the end of the world, of course, but if you want your poached eggs to be especially appealing, it's nice to nail the details.)

Fill a large, deep saucepan with about 8 inches (20cm) of water; your pan needs to be deep enough that when the egg is placed in it, it creates a teardrop shape. Bring the water to a gentle simmer over medium heat. Add a generous pinch of salt and a splash of white wine vinegar or white vinegar. (Salt helps make the water a little hotter while also seasoning the egg, and the vinegar helps the egg white coagulate so it holds its shape and results in a nice-looking finish.)

Crack each egg into a small ramekin or bowl to make sure it looks good and there's no shell in it. Stir the water somewhat vigorously to create a small whirl-pool and slide an egg gently into the center.

For large eggs, cook for 2 minutes 30 seconds for soft poached eggs or 4 minutes for firmer poached eggs. Use a slotted spoon to remove the finished eggs and drain them on paper towels. (If you don't plan to serve them immediately, you can stop the cooking by dropping the poached eggs gently into a bowl of ice water. To reheat them, simply place them in a pot of simmering water for a few seconds.)

SCRAMBLED EGGS

I learned how to make scrambled eggs at the Bentley hotel in London. We would crack six cartons of eggs into an extra-large bowl, create a bain-marie by placing the bowl over a huge pot of simmering water, and then whisk the eggs every so often for about an hour until they became velvety and smooth; then we added some butter to the scrambled eggs to finish them off. So, if you have an hour to spend babysitting eggs cooking over a bain-marie in the morning, go for it. But on the off-the-wall assumption that your mornings might be a bit hectic as you try to get yourself and possibly several other people ready for the day and out of the house, here's a quicker way to make smooth, velvety scrambled eggs that rival anything you'd get from a professional kitchen.

For a single serving, crack two eggs into a small saucepan or skillet. Add a generous pat of butter, a pinch of salt, and a few turns of ground black pepper. Place over medium heat and let cook undisturbed for about 20 seconds. Then, using a wooden spoon or similar tool, start to move the eggs around, stirring gently. (Some people like to add a few figure-eight patterns.)

I like my scrambled eggs to have a coarse texture, but if you prefer a finer texture, mix a bit more vigorously and frequently until they're cooked to your desired level of doneness. Eggs continue to cook a little more after they're off the heat, so I recommend adding another pat of butter and taking them off slightly before they're done to your liking.

Serve immediately. Feel free to top your eggs with a few scrapes of Parmesan cheese and a few slices of prosciutto or ham. Use chopped fresh basil leaves, a bit of shredded mozzarella cheese, and some oil-packed sun-dried tomatoes for a delicious breakfast with an Italian flair.

If you're cooking for more than one person, simply use more eggs and a larger pan, and note that the total cooking time will be longer.

BOILED EGGS

Whether you like them soft-boiled, hard-boiled, or something in-between, boiled eggs make excellent low-carb snacks. If you peel them ahead of time, they're great for grabbing and going when you're in a hurry and need some good protein and fat with nearly zero carbs. Put a few in a zip-top bag or sealed container and be on your way.

If cooking soft- or medium-boiled eggs, bring a medium-sized pot of water to a gentle simmer. Add the eggs and cook according to the following table. If cooking hard-boiled eggs, start the eggs in cold water. Bring to a gentle simmer and cook for 7 minutes 30 seconds after the water starts simmering. Precision is key; being off by just 30 seconds will make all the difference to your final product, so a timer is your friend. (*Note:* The times listed here are for large eggs.)

Style	Texture	Cooking Time
Soft-boiled	Slightly firm white; liquid yolk	4 minutes 30 seconds
Medium-boiled	Firm white; yolk mostly set	6 minutes 30 seconds
Hard-boiled	Firm white; yolk fully cooked	7 minutes 30 seconds

To keep your eggs at the perfect consistency and not overcook them, use a slotted spoon to remove them from the water as soon as the timer goes off and plunge them straight into a bowl of ice water. If you plan to serve them cold or refrigerate them to use later, you can keep them in the ice water for as long as you like. To serve them warm, remove them from the ice water after 30 seconds. The shells should crack and come off easily if you roll the eggs gently on a hard surface.

SOFT

MEDIUM

HARD

FRIED EGGS

You know about BLTs, right? Well, when I was a kid, my dad was famous for his TEBs—toasted egg and bacon sandwiches. After all these years, I still think of morning TEBs when I see a fried egg.

The key to a fried egg with a yolk that's rich and creamy and a firm white that's cooked but not crispy and dry is to start with a nonstick skillet over medium heat. Melt a generous pat of butter in the pan, then crack a fresh egg into the pan and gradually increase the heat. You don't want to overcook the white before the yolk is warmed through, so it's important not to let the pan get too hot too soon.

Cook the egg for 2 to 2½ minutes for a runny yolk. If you prefer a firmer yolk, flip the egg after 2 minutes and cook it for 1 minute longer. Season as desired. I like to keep it simple with Maldon salt and fresh ground black pepper, but any of the spice blends in this book will be wonderful here.

OMELETTE

This is not the overstuffed half-moon–shaped variety you might be used to from diners and specialty breakfast places. This is a more traditional French take on an omelette, pale on the outside and soft in the center. It takes some practice to get it right, but once you do, you'll never look back.

Start with three large eggs at room temperature. Beat well, seasoning to taste. (Use whatever seasonings you like, but simple salt and pepper go a long way in a classic dish like this.) Melt a pat of butter in a 9- or 10-inch (22 or 25cm) nonstick skillet over medium heat. Let the butter coat the bottom of the pan, then add the beaten eggs. Let the eggs cook undisturbed for 30 seconds so they begin to set. Then fold the two sides in toward the center and gently turn the omelette over so that the seam is on the bottom. Slide it onto a plate and serve immediately. The entire process should take no longer than 60 seconds.

EGG WRAPS

Just because you're not eating most forms of starch doesn't mean you're relegated to a life without wraps and tortillas. Egg wraps to the rescue! With the keto and low-carb ways of eating being so popular now, egg wraps are available in many grocery stores, but boy, are they pricey. Why pay a premium when you can make them yourself, easily, and at a fraction of the price?

There's just one ingredient: eggs! (Add salt and pepper if you want to get fancy. Better yet, use one of the spice blends in this book!)

Here's what to do to make one 8-inch (20cm) wrap:

1. Whisk a large egg (and seasoning, if using) in a bowl. Melt a pat of butter or heat a drizzle of oil in an 8-inch (20cm) nonstick skillet over medium heat. Let the fat coat the bottom of the pan and pour in the egg. Cook for 60 to 90 seconds on each side and, presto, they're done!

2. The wraps will keep covered in the fridge for up to 2 days. I like to fill mine with ham and cheese or, if I'm feeling really fancy, smoked salmon and cream cheese. Be creative!

Tip: Make sweet egg wraps! Add your preferred zero-carb sweetener, vanilla extract, and cinnamon, pumpkin pie spice, or another similar flavoring and cook as directed above. Use them as dessert crêpes!

CHICKEN BROTH

MAKES about
4 quarts/
4 liters (1 cup/
240ml per
serving)

A good chicken broth is the base for countless soups and stews; it can also be enjoyed on its own with a pinch of salt. Some people have a warm cup of broth instead of coffee or tea in the morning, and others drink it as a nightcap. Sure, you can buy canned or boxed broth from the store, but the flavor won't hold a candle to a batch you make yourself. If you appreciate nose-to-tail cooking, this is a great way to use a chicken even after you've eaten the meat. Next time you roast a chicken or cook pieces on the bone, save the carcass/ bones for this recipe and make it within a day or two (or freeze them for up to three months).

This broth freezes well. If you have extra freezer space—and a very large stockpot—and you think you will use the broth often, consider doubling the recipe. Chicken broth is quite low in carbs, fat, and protein since most of what you see on the ingredient list will be strained out.

6½ pounds (3kg) chicken
carcasses or bones

4 stalks celery

3 medium carrots

2 medium white onions

6 quarts (6 liters) cold water

10 peppercorns

4 sprigs fresh thyme

2 bay leaves

1. Preheat the oven to 425°F (220°C).

2. Place the chicken carcasses or bones on a rimmed baking sheet or in a large roasting pan and roast until well browned, about 30 minutes.

3. While the bones are roasting, chop the celery, carrots, and onions.

4. Remove the bones from the oven. If there's some rendered fat in the pan, pour it into a stockpot; if not, add a splash of vegetable oil. Put the pot over high heat. When the fat is hot, add the vegetables and cook until golden brown, 10 to 12 minutes.

5. Add the roasted bones and water to the pot, making sure the water fully covers all the ingredients. Bring to a boil, skimming off the excess fat that rises to the surface. Add the peppercorns, thyme, and bay leaves. Lower the heat and gently simmer, uncovered, for 3 to 4 hours. (You want the broth to have a rich flavor and to reduce to the point where it barely covers the bones; if it has reduced too much, top it up with cold water and heat it through, periodically skimming the fat from the top. This will ensure a clear broth. Alternatively, you can skim the fat after the broth is done and has cooled in the fridge. The fat will solidify on top and may be easier to remove.)

Nutrition per serving:		
Carb	Fat	Protein
	0.5g	
1.1g	(Most will be skimmed off.)	1.6g

6. Strain the broth through a fine-mesh strainer lined with a few layers of cheesecloth (this will ensure that any impurities are strained out). You may add salt at this point if you wish, or leave the broth as-is and season it when you use it for cooking or drinking.

7. Store extra broth in the freezer for up to 3 months.

BEEF BROTH

MAKES about
4 quarts/
4 liters (1 cup/
240ml per
serving)

Beef broth is the foundation for so many fabulous savory, hearty, and nourishing dishes. A cup of this, all by itself, is a nice pick-me-up on a cold winter day. Just like chicken broth, you can buy prepared beef broth at the store, but you'll do yourself and anyone you cook for a favor by taking the time to make it yourself. Consider making a double batch if you have a large enough stockpot and extra freezer space.

This may be a promise for some readers and a warning for others: your home will smell amazing from the time you start roasting the bones all the way through the cooking process. Be prepared for people to wander into the kitchen to see what's so enticing.

6½ pounds (3kg) beef marrow bones, preferably in 1-inch (2.5cm) pieces

4 stalks celery

3 medium carrots

2 medium white onions

6 quarts (6 liters) cold water

10 peppercorns

4 sprigs fresh thyme

2 bay leaves

1. Preheat the oven to 425°F (220°C).

2. Put the bones on a rimmed baking sheet or in a large roasting pan and roast until nice and brown, about 40 minutes.

3. While the bones are roasting, chop the celery, carrots, and onions.

4. Remove the bones from the oven. Some fat will have rendered out from the bones. Put a generous spoonful of this fat in a stockpot and cook the vegetables over high heat until golden brown, 10 to 12 minutes.

5. Add the roasted bones and water to the pot, making sure the water fully covers all the ingredients. Bring to a boil, skimming off the excess fat that rises to the surface. Add the peppercorns, thyme, and bay leaves. Lower the heat and gently simmer, uncovered, for 3 to 4 hours. (You want the broth to have a rich flavor and to reduce to the point where it barely covers the bones; if it has reduced too much, top it up with cold water and heat it through, periodically skimming the fat from the top. This will ensure a clear broth. Alternatively, you can skim the fat after the broth is done and has cooled in the fridge. The fat will solidify on top and may be easier to remove.)

Nutrition per serving:		
Carb	Fat	Protein
1.1g	0.5g (Most will be skimmed off.)	1.6g

6. Strain the broth through a fine-mesh strainer lined with a few layers of cheesecloth (this will ensure that any impurities are strained out). You may add salt at this point if you wish, or leave the broth as-is and season it when you use it for cooking or drinking.

7. Store extra broth in the freezer for up to 3 months.

ALL-PURPOSE BRINE

MAKES
3½ quarts
(3.5 liters)

This brine can be used for most meat, including pork and poultry. The quantities listed make enough brine for 1 large bird or 1 medium-sized slab of pork belly. If using larger meats, just double the recipe.

1 cup (275g) salt

20 peppercorns

10 sprigs fresh thyme

4 bay leaves

4 pods star anise

3½ quarts (3.5 liters) water

1. Put all the ingredients in a pot and place over high heat. Stir well. As soon as the salt has dissolved, remove the pot from the heat.

2. Let the brine cool completely before using.

Nutrition per serving:		
Carb	Fat	Protein
0g	0g	0g

SEASONING BLENDS

These are three of the seasoning blends I reach for all the time in my own kitchen. They're called for in some of the recipes in this book, but don't stop there. You can use these versatile flavorings anywhere you think they'll work well—most often in recipes of your own creation, I hope! Flavored salts and herb blends are the perfect way to jazz up any dish without adding carbs. Sure, you can find herb and spice blends at the store, but they often come with added sugar or other sweeteners and chemical agents to prevent caking. No thanks! When you make these blends yourself, you can control exactly what goes into them.

Rosemary Salt

MAKES about
1 cup/150g
(1 tablespoon/9g
per serving)

If you're a fan of lamb, this infused salt is for you! Earthy rosemary is the classic herb most often paired with lamb, but this fragrant herb works equally well with chicken, pork loin, and roasted vegetables. You could even try a pinch of it in egg salad. Such a great way to add more flavor to a dish without adding carbs.

1 heaping cup (150g) flaky or coarse salt, such as Maldon, pink, or kosher

2 tablespoons chopped fresh rosemary

1. Preheat the oven to 215°F (100°C).

2. Using a mortar and pestle or a mini food processor, blend together the salt and rosemary. Spread the mixture on a rimmed baking sheet and place in the oven to dry for 1 hour.

3. Allow the salt blend to cool before sealing it in an airtight container. It will keep for up to 1 month.

Nutrition per serving:		
Carb	Fat	Protein
0g	0g	0g

Smoky Chili and Garlic Salt

MAKES about
1 cup/150g
(1 tablespoon/9g
per serving)

Use this smoky, garlicky, spicy blend for anything you grill indoors or out—beef, pork, chicken, or fish. It also makes a great garnish for deviled eggs or a very light sprinkle on an omelette (see page 261). Smoked flaky salt can be found online or at specialty food stores. If you can't find chipotle powder, look for another smoked red chili; you want one with a smoky flavor rather than heat.

1 clove garlic, peeled

1 heaping cup (150g) smoked flaky salt

1 tablespoon chipotle powder

1. Preheat the oven to 215°F (100°C).

2. If using a mortar and pestle, combine the garlic, salt, and chipotle powder in the mortar and grind into a fine paste. If not, press the garlic with a garlic press into a fine paste, then put it in a small food processor. Add the salt and chipotle powder and blend into a fine paste.

3. Spread the mixture on a rimmed baking sheet and place in the oven for 1 hour, until thoroughly dry. The drying process will remove any excess moisture that would lead to the garlic spoiling.

4. Allow the salt blend to cool before sealing it in an airtight container. It will keep for up to 1 month.

Nutrition per serving:		
Carb	Fat	Protein
0.1g	0g	0g

Super Seasoning Blend

MAKES
¾ cup/110g
(1 tablespoon/9g
per serving)

I developed this recipe over many years, tinkering with the ingredients and amounts until it was just right. I consider it an all-purpose seasoning blend, and I reach for it so often that I like to have a big supply on hand all the time. It'll wake up the dullest food and breathe life into it; some specific applications are for roasted pork belly, deviled eggs, roasted chicken, or a large beef or pork roast. And don't forget vegetables—when roasting a pan of just about any kind of vegetable, toss them with olive oil and a generous bit of this seasoning before they go in the oven. You'll use just a pinch or a few shakes at a time, so one batch will last you a while, but feel free to double or triple the recipe if you often cook for a crowd.

---

3 tablespoons smoked paprika

2 tablespoons garlic powder

1 tablespoon celery salt

1 tablespoon ginger powder

1 tablespoon ground cumin

1 tablespoon mustard powder

1 tablespoon onion powder

1 tablespoon smoked salt

1 tablespoon fresh ground black pepper (or cayenne pepper for a spicy version)

Mix everything together well and store in an airtight container. When stored in a cool, dry, dark place, it will keep for about a month.

Nutrition per serving:		
Carb	Fat	Protein
0.5g	0g	0g

APPENDIXES

APPENDIX A:
ADAPT YOUR LIFE® ACADEMY

About the Academy

Dr. Westman has spent more than two decades conducting and publishing research establishing the beneficial impact of ketogenic and low-carb diets across an array of health issues, including type 2 diabetes, obesity, PCOS, and GERD. He created Adapt Your Life Academy to make trustworthy, science-backed education accessible to people far beyond the patients able to visit his clinic in person.

The Adapt Your Life Academy online courses are intended to help people implement ketogenic and low-carb diets in a simple, straightforward, and effective way while being free of the overcomplication and alarmism that accompany many other approaches. In addition to Dr. Westman's flagship Keto Made Simple Masterclass, the Academy offers courses on other diet and lifestyle issues taught by experts in their fields, including medical doctors, researchers, and other allied health professionals. In the near future, the Academy's offerings also include a culinary course taught by Chef Scott Parker, the author of this book. The course delivers Chef Scott's expert techniques to people's home kitchens to ensure students can implement what they've learned in a practical, sustainable way.

Adapt Your Life Academy's mission is to guide people in transforming their health and reclaiming their vitality by helping them execute simple but effective strategies for losing weight and reversing chronic diseases.

For more information about the Adapt Your Life Academy courses, visit adaptyourlifeacademy.com.

Carb Threshold Quiz

Are you brand-new to the ketogenic or low-carb way of eating? If you don't know which phase of the Adapt Your Life Diet is right for you, visit the Adapt Your Life Academy website and take the carb threshold quiz. This self-assessment will help you identify the level of carbohydrate intake that's best for you to start with.

adaptyourlifeacademy.com/carb-threshold-quiz/

APPENDIX B: FOOD LISTS

Adapt Your Life Phase 1 Food List

Food type	How much	What
Proteins	All you like until comfortably full but not stuffed	Beef, pork, lamb, bison, venison, chicken, turkey, duck, eggs (including yolks), finfish, shellfish (except oysters and clams), other animal proteins (game meats)
Salad vegetables	Up to 2 cups per day (measured uncooked)	Arugula, bok choy, cabbage (all varieties), chard, chives, endive, greens (beet, collard, mustard, and turnip greens), kale, lettuce (all varieties), parsley, radicchio, radishes, scallions, spinach, watercress
Nonstarchy vegetables	Up to 1 cup per day (measured uncooked)	Artichokes, asparagus, broccoli, Brussels sprouts, cauliflower, celery, celery root (celeriac), cucumber, eggplant (aubergine), fennel, green beans (string beans), jicama, kohlrabi, leeks, mushrooms, okra, onions, bell peppers (capsicum), other peppers (poblano, serrano, jalapeño, etc.), unsweetened pumpkin, rhubarb, shallots, snow peas, sprouts (bean and alfalfa), sugar-snap peas, summer squash, tomatoes, wax beans, zucchini (courgette)
Cheese	Up to 4 ounces per day	• Aged cheeses: Asiago, blue, Brie, Camembert, cheddar, Colby, Emmental, Gouda, Gruyère, Parmesan, provolone, Swiss, etc. • Soft fresh cheeses (goat cheese, mozzarella, cream cheese): check label for carb count
Added fats and oils	2-tablespoon maximum per day of each	• Mayonnaise • Butter, ghee, oils, heavy cream, sour cream • Oil-based salad dressings
Limited quantity foods	Maximums per day	• Soy sauce: 2 tablespoons • Lemon or lime juice: 2 tablespoons • Avocado: ½ fruit • Pickles (unsweetened): 2 servings • Olives: 6

Condiments	Stay under 20g total carbs per day for all your food	Mustard, vinegar (go easy on balsamic), unsweetened hot sauce, salsa, low-carb salad dressings (watch the total fat), fresh or dried herbs and spices
Zero-carb snacks	Unlimited within reason	Pork rinds, sugar-free fruit-flavored gelatin, pepperoni or salami slices, hard-boiled eggs, zero-sugar beef jerky
Fruit	None	—
Nuts and seeds	None	—
Beverages	Unlimited	Water, tea (hot or iced—no sugar), coffee (watch the amount of cream), sugar-free or unsweetened flavored drinks, diet soda, unsweetened flavored seltzer/sparkling water

Notes:

- The amounts listed are maximums to stay under, not minimums to aim for every day.

- These are the foods that are *permitted*, not that are *required*. You do not need to eat 2 cups of leafy greens and 1 cup of nonstarchy vegetables per day if you do not want to. You do not need to use added fats and oils if you are satisfied with the fat that comes naturally with your meat, poultry, cheese, and so on.

- Proteins: All cuts of meat are permitted—chops, roasts, steaks, ground meats, sausage (no sugar or starchy fillers), bacon, cured or processed meats (salami, pepperoni, lunchmeat—read labels for total carbs), all poultry cuts, organ meats.

- Seafood: Canned fish is permitted (tuna, salmon, sardines, mackerel); avoid imitation seafood.

- If you are trying to lose body fat, use added fats and oils sparingly. Enjoy the fat that occurs naturally in meat, seafood, poultry, eggs, and cheese. If you are living with a health problem but are not carrying excess body weight, you may consume larger quantities of fats and oils.

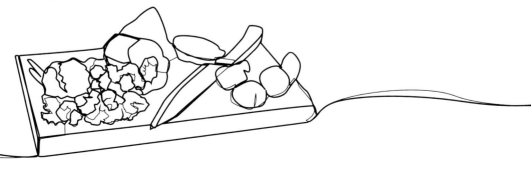

Adapt Your Life Phase 2 Food List

Food type	How much	What
Proteins	All you like until comfortably full but not stuffed	Beef, pork, lamb, bison, venison, chicken, turkey, duck, eggs (includes yolks), finfish, shellfish (except oysters and clams), other animal proteins (game meats)
Salad vegetables	4 cups per day (measured uncooked)	Arugula, bok choy, cabbage (all varieties), chard, chives, endive, greens (beet, collard, mustard, and turnip greens), kale, lettuce (all varieties), parsley, radicchio, radishes, scallions, spinach, watercress
Nonstarchy vegetables + Phase 2 vegetables	2 cups nonstarchy veg OR 1 cup nonstarchy veg plus 1 cup Phase 2 veg (measured uncooked) per day	• Nonstarchy: Artichokes, asparagus, broccoli, Brussels sprouts, cauliflower, celery, celery root (celeriac), cucumber (includes nonsweet pickles), eggplant (aubergine), fennel, green beans (string beans), jicama, kohlrabi, leeks, mushrooms, okra, onions, peppers (bell, poblano, serrano, jalapeño, etc.), unsweetened pumpkin, rhubarb, shallots, snow peas, sprouts (bean and alfalfa), sugar-snap peas, summer squash, tomatoes, wax beans, zucchini (courgette) • Phase 2 vegetables: Beets, carrots, rutabaga, turnips, winter squash (acorn, butternut, Hubbard, spaghetti)
Cheese	4 ounces per day	All cheeses—fresh and aged; soft, semisoft, hard (read labels for carb count in processed cheese products)
Added fats and oils	Maximums per day	• Mayonnaise: 2 tablespoons • Butter, ghee, oils, heavy cream, sour cream: 3 tablespoons • Oil-based salad dressings: 2 tablespoons
Limited quantity foods	Maximums per day	• Soy sauce: 3 tablespoons • Avocado: 1 fruit • Olives: 12
Condiments	Stay under 50g total carbs per day for all your food	Mustard, vinegar (go easy on balsamic), unsweetened hot sauce, salsa, sugar-free ketchup, low-carb salad dressings (watch the total fat), lemon/lime juice, fresh or dried herbs and spices
Zero-carb snacks	Unlimited within reason	Pork rinds, sugar-free fruit-flavored gelatin, pepperoni or salami slices, hard-boiled eggs, zero-sugar beef jerky
Fruit	½ cup berries or 1 small to medium fruit per day	Apricots, blackberries, blueberries, cranberries (fresh and unsweetened, not dried), nectarines, peaches, plums, raspberries, strawberries
Nuts and seeds	2 ounces per day	All nuts and seeds (go easy on higher-carb items: peanuts, cashews, pistachios)
Dairy	Maximums per day*	• Plain or sugar-free flavored yogurt: 1 cup • Cottage cheese: 1 cup • Ricotta cheese: ½ cup
Low-carb grain products	See note*	Low-carb, high-fiber crispbreads, crackers, wraps, flatbreads

*Keep your portions to sizes that allow you to stay under 50 grams of total carbs per day for all your food.

Notes:

- The amounts listed are maximums to stay under, not minimums to aim for every day.

- These are the foods that are permitted, not that are required. You do not need to eat 4 cups of leafy greens and 2 cups of nonstarchy vegetables per day if you do not want to. You do not need to use added fats and oils if you are satisfied with the fat that comes naturally with your meat, poultry, cheese, and so on.

- Proteins: All cuts of meat are permitted—chops, roasts, steaks, ground meats, sausage (no sugar), bacon, cured or processed meats (salami, pepperoni, lunchmeat—read labels for total carbs), all poultry cuts, organ meats.

- Seafood: Canned fish is permitted (tuna, salmon, sardines, mackerel); avoid imitation seafood.

Adapt Your Life Phase 3 Food List

Food type	How much	What
Proteins	All you like until comfortably full but not stuffed	Beef, pork, lamb, bison, venison, chicken, turkey, duck, eggs (includes yolks), finfish, shellfish, other animal proteins (game meats)
Salad vegetables	Unlimited (but stay under 150g total carbs per day)	Arugula, bok choy, cabbage (all varieties), chard, chives, endive, greens (beet, collard, mustard, and turnip greens), kale, lettuce (all varieties), parsley, radicchio, radishes, scallions, spinach, watercress
Other vegetables	Unlimited*	Artichokes, asparagus, avocado, beets, broccoli, Brussels sprouts, carrots, cauliflower, celery, celery root (celeriac), cucumber, eggplant (aubergine), fennel, green beans (string beans), jicama, kohlrabi, leeks, mushrooms, okra, olives, onions, parsnips, peppers (bell, poblano, serrano, jalapeño, etc.), pumpkin, rhubarb, rutabaga, shallots, snow peas, sprouts (bean and alfalfa), sugar-snap peas, summer squash, tomatoes, turnips, wax beans, winter squash (acorn, butternut, Hubbard, spaghetti), zucchini (courgette)
Starchy root vegetables	1 medium to large per day or 1-serving equivalent	Sweet potatoes, white potatoes, yams, yuca/cassava
Cheese and other dairy	Use high-fat dairy sparingly if weight is a concern	• All cheeses—fresh and aged; soft, semisoft, hard: 5 ounces • Plain or sugar-free flavored yogurt: 1 to 2 cups • Cottage cheese: 1 to 2 cups
Added fats and oils	Maximums per day (use less if weight is a concern)	• Mayonnaise: 3 tablespoons • Butter, ghee, oils, heavy cream, sour cream: 4 tablespoons • Oil-based salad dressings: 4 tablespoons
Condiments	See note*	Mustard, vinegar, unsweetened hot sauce, salsa, salad dressings, lemon/lime juice, sugar-free ketchup, fresh or dried herbs and spices
Zero-carb snacks	Unlimited within reason	Pork rinds, sugar-free fruit-flavored gelatin, pepperoni or salami slices, hard-boiled eggs, zero-sugar beef jerky
Fruit	See note*	All fruits (favor fresh, whole fruit over canned or dried)
Nuts and seeds	4 ounces per day	All nuts and seeds
Beans, legumes, and pulses	1 to 2 cups*	All beans, legumes, and pulses: black beans, edamame, garbanzos, green peas, kidney, lentils, lima, navy, turtle, etc.
Grains	1 to 2 cups*	Amaranth, barley, buckwheat, corn, millet, oats, quinoa, rice, spelt, wheat, other grains

*Keep your portions to sizes that allow you to stay under 150 grams of total carbs per day for all your food.

Notes:

- No foods are off-limits for Phase 3 except sugar. Keep your total carbohydrate intake for the day to 150 grams or fewer. Consume more carbs on hard training days if needed.

- The amounts listed are maximums to stay under, not minimums to aim for every day.

- These are the foods that are permitted, not that are required. You do not need to eat large amounts of vegetables or to consume starchy vegetables, beans, or grains if you do not want to. You do not need use a lot of added fats and oils if you are satisfied with the fat that comes naturally with your meat, poultry, eggs, cheese, etc.

- Proteins: All cuts of meat are permitted—chops, roasts, steaks, ground meats, sausage (no sugar), bacon, cured or processed meats (salami, pepperoni, lunchmeat—read labels for total carbs), all poultry cuts, organ meats.

- Seafood: Canned fish is permitted (tuna, salmon, sardines, mackerel).

APPENDIX C: MEASUREMENT EQUIVALENTS

Note: I am a native Brit currently living in South Africa. I developed the recipes for this book using metric measurements and then converted them to U.S. measurements. When in doubt, please default to the metric measurement. As noted in the Introduction, a food scale for weighing ingredients is a very helpful tool, especially when following a low-carb or ketogenic diet.

Liquid Volume

1 teaspoon			5ml
3 teaspoons	1 tablespoon		15ml
2 tablespoons	⅛ cup	1 fluid ounce	30ml
4 tablespoons	¼ cup	2 fluid ounces	60ml
5⅓ tablespoons	⅓ cup	3 fluid ounces	80ml
8 tablespoons	½ cup	4 fluid ounces	120ml
16 tablespoons	1 cup	8 fluid ounces	240ml
1 pint	2 cups	16 fluid ounces	480ml
1 quart	4 cups	32 fluid ounces	1 liter

Weight

Ounces	Pounds	Grams
1 ounce	¹⁄₁₆ pound	30g
4 ounces	¼ pound	120g
8 ounces	½ pound	240g
12 ounces	¾ pound	360g
16 ounces	1 pound	480g*

*In this book, the equivalent of 500g is used for 1 pound based on how food products tend to be sold outside the U.S.

Length

Inches	Millimeters/Centimeters
¼ inch	6mm
½ inch	12mm
1 inch	2.5cm
6 inches	15cm
12 inches	30cm

Oven Temperature

Fahrenheit	Celsius
325°F	160°C
350°F	180°C
375°F	190°C
400°F	200°C
425°F	220°C
450°F	230°C

Butter

	American (1 Cup/ 2 Sticks)	European (1 Package)
Weight	227g	250g*
Fat Content	184g	205g*

*These numbers are for unsalted butter. I prefer to use unsalted butter in all of my cooking because it gives me far greater control when seasoning dishes.

ACKNOWLEDGMENTS

This book is a reflection not just of me and my cooking, but the work of a whole team that came together with the goal of changing and saving lives through delicious food. It took a chef, a doctor, a writer, and food photographers and stylists, not to mention my incredible butcher, to make this a reality, and I want to thank them all here.

First, a thank you to all the chefs I have worked under who taught me all I know and helped me become the chef I am today. To Andrew Turner at the Bentley, for teaching me everything I needed to know about getting into the world of fine dining and perfecting eggs. To Shane Osborne at Pied à Terre, for taking a chance on me as a student and teaching me some incredible skills, from baking bread to cooking fish to butchery—skills I use today and continue to attempt to perfect. Then, of course, to Claude Bosi, for taking me on and making me your junior sous—a year that was one of the hardest in my career—and for trusting me in a senior role to help earn back that second star. The trip to Noma with you will forever be one of my fondest memories. Having the opportunity to cook with you and some of the world's other great chefs was truly a young chef's dream come true. And last but certainly not least, to Daniel Clifford, for giving me the richest opportunity in my professional life, running your restaurant, a place you have worked your life to build. You inspire me every day, and your relentless hard work and passion will stick with me forever. I wish I could be there when you get your third star!

To Dr. Eric Westman and Glen Finkel: We started working together in early 2021, after you approached me to create recipes suitable for a very-low-carb diet. (And to be on video making them, to boot!) Many of those recipes are included in this book, and I am honored to think that they may play some small role in helping people enjoy truly delicious and nourishing food while restoring them back to health. Dr. Westman, your life's work is inspiring and admirable, and Glen, your energy and ambition to accomplish big things are contagious. Thanks also to nutritionist and author Amy Berger for writing and editing assistance.

Thank you to my incredible photographer and food stylist, Marguerite Oelofse and Ellen Schwerdtfeger. What a great two weeks we had capturing these incredible images. (If I try hard enough, I think I can smell the pictures!) I had an idea of what I wanted the book to look like, and you both far exceeded my expectations. And I would be remiss if I didn't thank Jared Hohne for keeping my hair fresh.

Thanks, of course, to my wife and family. Shona, you have been incredibly patient with me over the years, and I know it wasn't easy to have your home taken over by two weeks of professional food styling! You are my rock, and I love you. My love to all the rest of my family for your support and input, and to my dad in particular—the book wouldn't be complete without your Singapore noodle recipe. To Uncle Mark, for getting me my first job in London with Roy, and then all the great jobs we did together after.

My gratitude to Le Creuset and Mervyn Gers for your generosity in providing the highest quality and most attractive cookware and plates. We eat with our eyes first, and your fabulous products helped showcase my recipes and turn them into a visual feast as well as a delight for the palate.

And last, but by no means least, good food needs to come from somewhere, and I'm fortunate to have Ryan Boon not only as my butcher but even more as my friend. Thank you, Ryan, for the incredible meat that's featured in this book, and for being an integral part of my education about quality meats and the fine art of butchery.

—Scott

RECIPE INDEX

BREAKFAST

38
Prosciutto, Cheese, and Veggie Egg Roll

40
Breakfast Stack

42
Poached Eggs with Feta on Cheese and Chive Toast

44
Smoked Salmon Omelette

46
Eggs in Spiced Tomatoes

48
Breakfast Egg Bites

50
Broccoli and Feta Frittata

APPETIZERS AND SNACKS

54
Beef and Zucchini Frikkadels

56
Crispy Chicken Wings

58
Two-Minute Cheese and Chive Rolls

60
Marinated Feta Cheese

62
Pan-Seared Halloumi

64
Dressed Olives

66
Toasted Sesame Cabbage Snacks

68
Kale Chips

SALADS AND SOUPS

72

Warm Kale and
Blue Cheese Salad
with Walnuts
and Bacon

74

Bacon-y
Caesar Salad

76

Tomato Salad
with Burrata,
Herbs, and Poppy
Seeds

78

Goat Cheese,
Red Cabbage,
Green Bean, and
Almond Salad

80

Chargrilled
Zucchini with
Crispy Halloumi
and Kale Pesto

82

Barley Salad with
Marinated Feta,
Peas, and Mint

84

Orange, Celery,
and Fennel Salad
with Blue Cheese
and Pumpkin
Seeds

86

Broccoli, Spinach,
and Stilton Soup

88

Cauliflower
Cheese and
Pancetta Soup

MAIN DISHES

92
Stuffed Roasted Zucchini with Tomato and Herb Salsa

94
Foil-Wrapped Salmon with Cumin-Spiced Cauliflower Rice

96
Soy-Cured Salmon with Fennel and Cucumber Salad

98
Zoodle Carbonara

100
Dad's Singapore Zoodles

104
Pan-Fried NY Strip Steak with Charred Green Beans, Arugula, and Quick-Pickled Scallions

106
Beef Tacos in Lettuce Cups with Lime Crema

108
Black Pepper Chicken Ramen

110
Seared Tuna with Avocado, Cucumber, and Tomato Salad

112
Garlic Prawns

114
Crispy Chicken Leg Quarters with Sesame, Soy, and Leafy Greens

116
Pan-Seared Lamb Chops with Roasted Vegetables and Yogurt Mint Sauce

118
Kung Pao Chicken

120
Cottage Pie

124
Zucchini Lasagna

126
Moussaka

130
Peri-Peri Chicken

132
Pot-au-Feu

134
Bacon and Brie Burgers with Zesty Toppings

136
Smoked Haddock with Hollandaise and Fennel Butter Cabbage

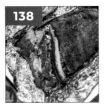
138
Slow-Cooked Pork Ribs

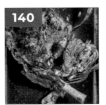
140
Roasted Rosemary and Garlic Leg of Lamb

142
Asparagus with Prosciutto, Poached Egg, and Arugula

144
Calamari with Chorizo

146
Ruby Murray Chicken Curry

148
Zoodle Bolognese

150
Fish Pie

152
Mediterranean Trout with Crushed Peas and Tomato-Radish Salsa

154
Sea Bass with Lemon Butter and Mashed Broccoli

156
Five-Minute Salmon

158
Tortilla Pizza

160
Fish Carpaccio with Radish and Smashed Avocado

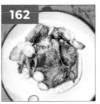
162
Pork Chops with Braised Cabbage and Mustard-Cheese Sauce

164
Spicy Meatballs in Roasted Tomato Sauce

166
Moules Marinières

168
Rosemary Baked Chicken with Green Beans and Tomatoes

SIDE DISHES

172
Cauliflower
Mash

174
Broccoli
Mash

176
Cauliflower
Rice

178
Cauliflower
Steaks

180
Red Cabbage
Slaw

182
Roasted Carrots

184
Roasted
Butternut Mash

186
Roasted Sweet
Potato Mash

188
Smashed
Cucumber Salad

190
Quick-Pickled
Onions

192
Kimchi

DIPS, DRESSINGS, SAUCES, AND SPREADS

198
Four-Cheese
Sauce or Dip

200
Brown Butter
Hollandaise

202
Blue Cheese Dip

204
Sour Cream and
Chive Dip

206
Horseradish
Cream Sauce

208

Homemade
Mayonnaise

210

Japanese-
Inspired Dressing

212

Simple
Salad Dressing

214

Kale Pesto

216

Crème Fraîche
Dill and Onion
Sauce

218

Roasted
Tomato Sauce

220

Smoky Lime and
Chili Butter

222

Lemon,
Black Pepper,
and Garlic Butter

THE FOUNDATIONS

226

The Perfect Steak

238

The Perfect
Pork Belly

240

The Perfect
Chicken

248

The Perfect Fish

252

The Perfect Egg

264

Chicken Broth

266

Beef Broth

268

All-Purpose Brine

271

Rosemary Salt
and Smoky Chili
and Garlic Salt

272

Super Seasoning
Blend

GENERAL INDEX